THE
Baseball Fan's
COMPANION

**How to Master the Subtleties of the World's
Most Complex Team Sport and Learn
to Watch the Game Like an Expert**

NICK BAKALAR

MACMILLAN • USA

MACMILLAN
A Simon & Schuster Macmillan Company
1633 Broadway
New York, NY 10019-6785

Book Design by George J. McKeon

Library of Congress Cataloging-in-Publication Data available upon request

ISBN 0-02-860848-8

Manufactured in the United States of America
10 9 8 7 6 5 4 3 2 1

For Elizabeth,
Eliz, Liz, Lizzie, Libby—by whatever name, the best.

Acknowledgments

I would like to thank Jim Charlton, for sharing his wealth of knowledge about the game and its history and for saving me from several embarrassing errors; Jonathan Schwartz, who allowed me to borrow a bit of his baseball eloquence; Paul Bresnick and Les Pockell, old comrades in arms, who read and gave me valuable comments on several chapters; Karen McKinnon, who knows statistics—really knows them, and not just baseball statistics, either; Marty Cooper, Alice Cooper, and especially David Cooper, who knows much more about baseball (and, I suspect, about much else) than his modest manner allows him to admit; and John Thorn, whose baseball wisdom is exceeded only by his generosity. Thanks to the Macmillan team, made up of Ken Samelson, Jeanine Bucek, and Patty Shaw. And of course, the heart of it all, Traci Cothran, my editor.

My brothers, Ken and Jake Bakalar, read the manuscript with great care, made numerous useful suggestions, and corrected many errors with unfailing good grace. Therefore, I really don't see why these two shouldn't be blamed for whatever deficiencies remain.

Contents

Introduction

In 1951, the Dodgers played the Giants in a three-game playoff for the National League Championship and the right to face the Yankees in the World Series. Even casual baseball fans know what happened: In the third game, in the bottom of the ninth inning with one out, the Giants' Bobby Thomson hit a home run to win the game and the pennant. That home run is now legendary. The films and photographs of Thomson's shot, the Giants' ecstatic celebration, the Dodgers' dejected skulk toward their clubhouse, and the near-hysterical voice of the radio announcer Russ Hodges are now icons of baseball history. It has become one of those events that millions of people claim to have witnessed—probably including some who weren't even born in 1951. The story has been told so often that it would seem there is nothing to add to it.

But there is one detail that may have been missed even by those lucky enough to have been present that day. When Thomson hit the homer, and the radio announcer went ballistic, and the Giants celebrated, and the Dodgers sulked, and the fans poured out onto the field—while all this was going on—one man kept concentrating on the game. Dodger second baseman Jackie Robinson watched Thomson intently, waiting to see if he would miss a base and invalidate his homer. Of course, Thomson touched them all, and no matter how many times Brooklyn fans watch those films, it always comes out the same. But this proves two things about Jackie Robinson: First, that he was one of the greatest competitors the game has ever known. And second, that he always—always—had his head in the game.

Every batter, every situation, forces a ballplayer to consider a complex combination of possibilities and to construct alternative plans of action to respond to each of them. As the game progresses, the number of possibilities and their complexity increase. If a ballplayer isn't thinking, but just relying on his physical skills (however prodigious they may be), he isn't playing good baseball. In fact, in a sense, if a ballplayer isn't thinking he isn't really playing baseball at all; and if a fan isn't thinking, he or she isn't really watching it. In baseball, even the spectators have to have their heads in the game.

> *"The trouble with baseball is by the time you learn how to play it, you can't play it any more."*
> —FRANK HOWARD

One way to make sure that you're keeping your head in the game is to keep score in writing. It used to be that you "couldn't tell the players without a scorecard"—that is, to identify players on the field, you needed a list of their names and numbers. But the giant message boards that provide names, numbers, and even some statistics, plus the 100-foot television screens that offer color photos and instant replays—amenities in almost every major league ball-park—have given that phrase the quaint sound it now has. In fact, you can very easily tell the players without a scorecard. But a game can be a lot more interesting if you do keep a scorecard in your hands.

In every team sport, someone—usually an assistant coach—is constantly writing something down: assists and rebounds, shots on goal, saves, sacks, whatever. But in baseball, there are many more numbers to keep track of. In fact, every pitch a pitcher makes is recorded on a piece of paper, usually by the pitcher who is starting the following day. You can see this happening: Tomorrow's pitcher is

The 1951 playoff game between the Dodgers and the Giants. Look carefully: Both umpires are staring directly at home plate, making sure Thomson touches it to make his home run official. Robinson is staring right along with them. If Thomson, in the excitement, had failed to touch home, Robinson would have been ready to appeal it. The other Dodgers in the picture—pitcher Ralph Branca and catcher Rube Walker—are too busy feeling disappointed to keep their heads in the game.   *National Baseball Library & Archive, Cooperstown, NY*

the guy sitting on the steps of the dugout with the clipboard in his hand, furiously writing. This is called *charting the pitches*. At the end of the game, there will be a record of how many pitches, and what kind, each pitcher has thrown—this in addition to the records of what every batter has done in every time at bat.

> "More than any other American sport, baseball creates the magnetic, addictive illusion that it can almost be understood."
> —TOM BOSWELL

Very few fans would want to score in that much detail. A somewhat larger number will want to learn the conventions of scoring—the symbols and abbreviations used to indicate what has happened to each batter. Published forms are available for this, all divided into neat little boxes, with diagrams of the field in each box and lists of hitters' results to be checked off, plus spaces for recording the count on the batter. These forms are available in sporting goods stores. Coaches and announcers use them, but you don't need an elaborate form to score a game. All you need is a piece of paper divided into a grid with the batters listed down the left side of the grid and the innings across the top, a few symbols and abbreviations, and a constant attention to what's happening on the field.

The abbreviations you need to know to score a game are as follows. Each position has a number: 1. Pitcher; 2. Catcher; 3. First baseman; 4. Second baseman; 5. Third baseman; 6. Shortstop; 7. Left fielder; 8. Center fielder; and 9. Right fielder. *K* means a strikeout; a backwards *K* is on a called strikeout. *BB* is a base on balls. *DP* is a double play. *F* stands for a fly-out. So when a player grounds a ball to the third baseman, who then throws to first base to get him out, you write 5–3 in the box and draw a little circle with a 1 inside it to indicate the first out of the inning.

But it's easy enough to elaborate with your own system of symbols. Consider the four corners of the box to be the four bases.

Draw a line in the corner representing first base when a player gets a single; add a line in the next corner if he makes it to second. Color in the whole box if he crosses the plate safely, so you can see at a glance how many runs have been scored. Invent a symbol for a pickoff or a caught stealing. Write it in the box when the event occurs, indicating what base it happened at and where the ball went. At the end of the inning, add up the hits and runs, and write them at the bottom of the column. Looking back at your scorecard, you'll be able to picture each play, remembering and savoring all the details.

Try it next time you're at the park. Watch the accumulation of information as the game progresses. See how the pitcher is doing inning to inning. With this record in hand, you can develop a coherent picture of the game that doesn't emerge if you're just watching one hitter, one play at a time. You will see patterns emerge from the numbers, like how many pitches a pitcher can throw before his arm tires or what place in the outfield a batter tends to hit. We should add a health warning: If you begin to do this early enough in life, it can become seriously addictive.

Now every fan loves to see a home run, or an overpowering pitching performance, or a close play at the plate. But baseball holds deeper pleasures if you know how to look for them. Looking for them requires attention; knowing what to look for requires the understanding of some of the game's subtleties. Even a lifetime spent in baseball will not teach a person everything about the game, but every casual fan can learn how to enjoy the game at a higher level. That's what this book will help you do.

> *"In baseball, you don't know nothing."*
> —YOGI BERRA

Do you know what constitutes a balk? Do you know why it is that when a runner misses a base, the other team has to appeal the play to the umpire before he'll call it? Do you understand the difference between a slider and a curve? Are you puzzled when a manager brings a pitcher into a game to pitch to one batter and then pulls him out? Do you know what a double switch is, and when a manager might use it? Did you ever notice that one part of the catcher's job is to back up first base on certain plays? What's a cutoff man, and why is it important to "hit" him on a throw from the outfield? Why is the infield pulled in on one play, and then back on the next? Knowing the answers to these questions and more makes the difference between spending a couple of enjoyable hours at the ballpark and appreciating the subtle rules, moves, strategies, and techniques that make baseball the most intricate, elegant, and complex team sport there is.

By reading this book, I hope, you'll understand why the big home run, the stolen base, the overpowering 15-strikeout performance, and the pennant-winning victory are only part of the fun of baseball. There are profound pleasures in watching a pair of second-division teams in mid-September when there is nothing at stake except good baseball. This book will give you the tools to appreciate and enjoy that otherwise "insignificant" ball game as much as you enjoy the seventh game of the World Series.

It Ain't Cheatin' if You Don't Get Caught: The Rules

1.01. Baseball is a game between two teams of nine players each, under the direction of a manager, played on an enclosed field in accordance with these rules, under jurisdiction of one or more umpires.

1.02. The objective of each team is to win by scoring more runs than the opponent.

1.03. The winner of the game shall be that team which shall have scored, in accordance with these rules, the greater number of runs at the conclusion of a regulation game.

So begins the book called *Official Baseball Rules*. Every manager has a copy of the book. So do most players. Every umpire carries a copy in his pocket (or at least keeps one nearby) during every game, just in case he needs to look something up or point something out to a doubting participant. Although the rules of baseball have been evolving for more than 125 years, the current version of the book was adopted in 1949 and has been revised some forty times since then. The Book (as we'll call it from now on, just so we know which book we're talking about) is written and revised by a committee of twelve called the Official Playing Rules Committee. It is available in pamphlet form, 104 pages long, and anyone can buy one in a bookstore for about four bucks. The Book includes commentaries on many of the rules and examples of how the more complicated ones work during a game. It also offers little lessons in life, like the passage in "General Instructions to Umpires" that reads "Keep your eye everlastingly on the ball while it is in play"; or the reminder that "Umpire dignity is important, but never as important as 'being right'"; or the concluding advice to "Finally, be courteous, impartial and firm, and so compel respect from all."

No one in the history of the universe ever learned to play baseball by reading the *Official Baseball Rules*. You learn to play baseball by playing it and watching it. But even people who've played and watched and watched some more don't necessarily know all the rules or how to interpret them. Here's a quick tour of The Book—just to remind you of a few points and maybe to show you a new wrinkle or two.

THE FIELD AND THE EQUIPMENT

Nine men on a team, nine innings, three outs, three bases plus home plate. When Alexander Cartwright codified the rules of baseball in 1846, he specified that second base should be 42 paces from home plate. If a man of average height takes 42 brisk paces, he walks just about 127 feet. Whether Cartwright knew or cared that the square of the hypotenuse is equal to the sum of the squares of the other two sides, 127.27922 feet is precisely the diagonal of a square that measures 90 feet on a side. Cartwright never stipulated 90 feet between bases—it just worked out that way. And for nearly 150 years, although everything else has changed in larger or smaller ways, that distance between bases has remained exactly the same. Although

I haven't tested the theory, I'll bet that if people of smaller physical stature—a team of women, for example, or one of Little Leaguers—were to have one of their members walk off those 42 paces, they would come up with a distance between bases as perfectly suited to their size, speed, and throwing ability as the 90 feet distance is to that of professional baseball players.

> *"It gets late early out there."*
>
> —Yogi Berra, elucidating certain theoretical considerations in solar astronomy with possible implications for ubiety in left field in Yankee Stadium during the period immediately following the autumnal equinox

The Book says that the line from home plate running through the pitcher's mound to second base should preferably run east-northeast. In the afternoon, then, the sun is at the batter's back, and the fielders play with the sun in their faces. Most major league fields are still laid out so that you're facing more or less east-northeast when you stand at the plate; but direction is irrelevant in covered stadiums. Some people, like those who built the Texas Rangers' stadium in Arlington, just don't respect the old ways. Before the arrival of domed stadiums and the predominance of night games, of course, this was more significant. In fact, as World Series time approaches in early fall, the angle of the sun is lower, making the layout even more important. When the World Series was played in the daytime, the *sun field*—left field—was critical. OK, now, everybody get out your straightedge and compass for today's quiz: Why are left-handed pitchers called *southpaws*?

The other dimensions of the infield are also specified precisely in The Book—the pitcher's mound is a certain diameter and height; the batter's box has precisely delineated dimensions; the pitcher's plate, or *rubber*, is exactly 60 feet 6 inches from home plate. The coaches' boxes where the first and third base coaches stand and the on-deck circle where the next batter stands or kneels are carefully prescribed in size and location. But when it comes to the outfield, there's quite a bit of variation. There were early rules about minimum distances; 250 feet was the nearest a fence could be to home plate until 1958, when the minimum (for newly built or newly renovated stadiums only) became 325 feet. The famous short right field in Yankee Stadium—it was 296 feet before they moved it back in the 1970s—was supposed to be a great boon to left-handed home run hitters. But Roger Maris, in 1961, hit 31 of his 61 homers on the road. And Ruth hit only 28 of his 60 in Yankee Stadium. In the Polo Grounds, which was razed after the 1963 season, the distances to right and left fields were an incredible 257.5 and 279 feet (although dead center field was dead indeed for hitters—480 feet away).

The variations in the distances to the outfield walls and the little nooks, crannies, and irregularities that give old stadiums their character are coming back into fashion. For a while, newly built stadiums always had perfectly regular outfields—Veterans Stadium in Philadelphia, Skydome in Toronto, and Three Rivers Stadium in Pittsburgh are examples. Someone once aptly described these places as "fifteen million tons of pre-stressed concrete dropped in the middle of a fourteen-acre parking lot." But the trend now is retro: Camden Yards in Baltimore, which opened in 1992 and is by general agreement the best ballpark in the country, has an outfield that is asymmetrical, open to the weather, and covered with, of all things, grass.

The rules demand that the home team furnish covered benches for the players, and they specify the details of the construction and size of bats, balls, and gloves. The catcher's mitt gets special attention—it can't be more than 38 inches in circumference—and size limits for all of the fielders' gloves are indicated as well. Batting helmets are mandatory—all batters, all base runners, and the catchers have to wear them. This rule was put in The Book only in 1971, although many players had begun using helmets long before that. In fact, they were first used by the Brooklyn Dodgers in the early 1940s, and they'd been required in the American League since 1957. Players more afraid of being called sissy than of being beaned were allowed to use less-effective plastic inserts hidden under their caps. In 1974, the single earflap helmet became mandatory; and in 1983, the ones with double earflaps, long familiar among Little Leaguers, became mandatory for minor leaguers. In 1988, catchers were required to wear helmets, and for good measure, so were batboys and bat girls. The home team wears its white uniform. The visiting team wears a color other than white. You'll probably be able to make out the Nike insignia on many players' shoes, but you can't put ads for sneakers and soft drinks on your uniform—this is baseball, my friend, not tennis.

WHAT'S A BUNT?

The Book is well organized, and before it gets into the action, it defines its terms. The *strike zone* is the area over home plate between the knees and the middle of the batter's shirt in his normal stance. A *ball* is a pitch that does not enter this zone, and is not struck at by the batter. A *strike* is a ball struck at and missed, or not struck at but passing within the strike zone, or a foul ball with less than two strikes on the batter. Any ball bunted foul is a strike regardless of whether there are two strikes. A *foul ball* is a ball hit outside the white *foul lines* delineating the limits of the playing field. (A ball that is fair when it bounces in the infield and then goes into foul territory after it passes first or third base is still a fair ball. If a ball hits a base, it's fair no matter where it bounces.)

A *base* is one of four points that must be touched by a runner to score a run; a *base on balls* (or *walk*) is an award of first base to a batter who receives four pitches outside the strike zone. A *force play* is a play by which a runner loses his right to occupy a base because a batter has become a runner—you can't have two men on one base at the same time, so one of them is "forced" to move. He can be put out by having a fielder stand with the ball in his hand on the base to which he must run. Thus the *double play* in which a runner on first is forced to run to second, but doesn't make it there before the fielder stands on second base with the ball in his hand;

the fielder then throws to first in an attempt to retire the batter as well. If the throw reaches first base before the batter does, you have two outs on one play.

The force play, as The Book notes, may result in some confusion. The Book says that a *tag* is the action of a fielder in touching a base with his body while holding the ball, or the act of touching the runner with the ball. You have to remember that a force can be removed if the trailing runner is retired before the runner preceding him. For example, man on first, one out. The ball is hit to the first baseman, who steps on the base, retiring the batter. But now the runner doesn't have to run to second—first base is empty. So that runner has to be touched with the ball to be out—standing on second base with the ball in hand is no longer enough. It's also a little confusing when it comes to scoring runs when two are out: Here, you have to remember that if the third out is a force out, the run crossing the plate doesn't count. If the third out is not a force, however, it depends when the run crossed. The run counts if it crossed the plate before the (nonforced) out was made.

The fielder's *tag* is not to be confused with the runner's act of *tagging up*. On a fly ball with less than two out, a runner can advance to the next base even if the fly is caught—but he can only start running after it is caught. Thus he *tags up*—waits on the base— until the ball is caught and then takes off running.

Obstruction is the act of a fielder who, while not holding the ball and not in the act of fielding it, impedes the progress of a runner. In other words, catchers can block the plate and prevent the runner from reaching it—but only if they actually have the ball in their hands. The Book points out that a fielder might legally get in a runner's way if he is fielding a ball, but once he has missed it he's no longer in the act of fielding. So if the second baseman dives for a ball, misses it, and then lies there for the runner to trip over him, that's obstruction.

A *run, line drive, foul tip, pitch,* and *throw* are all explained in The Book. The distinction between a throw and a pitch is particularly important because, as we will see, pitching is subject to many more constraints than simply throwing. In any case, *pitching* is delivering a ball to the batter; *throwing* is delivering it to anyone else. Foul tips—where the pitched ball nicks the batter's bat and goes into foul territory—are strikes up until strike two. A foul tip by a batter with two strikes is only strike three if the ball is caught and the catcher holds on to the ball; otherwise, the batter stays alive at the plate. A *triple play* and a *squeeze play*—where you try to get a runner on third to score by bunting him in (see Chapter 3)—are defined.

The Book even tells umpires how to start the game, or resume action following a dead ball. And they don't shout "Play ball!"—at least not according to The Book. The correct command is simply, "Play"; and the implication (although The Book is too polite to say so) is that this "play ball" stuff is bush.

Finally, to answer the question posed at the beginning of this section, it's right there in black and white: A *bunt* is "a batted ball not swung at, but intentionally met with the bat and tapped slowly within the field."

WARMING UP, STARTING THE GAME, AND STOPPING IT

Lots of baseballs are used during a game—a dozen or two may fly into the stands and become the property of lucky spectators who catch them; many become nicked, smudged, or otherwise unusable; and occasionally the pitcher asks for a new ball just because he doesn't like the feel of the one he's been given. He can do this whenever he wants to. Although The Book says only that the home team should provide "at least one dozen reserve balls," the usual number is more like five dozen. These must be delivered in sealed packages with the league president's signature on it. Umpires break the seal, and then take the gloss off the new balls by rubbing them with mud. This is not the ordinary multipurpose mud that you used for pretty much everything when you were a kid—it's special mud from the banks of the Delaware River. Apparently it takes away the gloss without changing the color of the balls. Anyway, one of the umpires' jobs is to dirty up a bunch of balls with this mud before every game.

LEAST-OFTEN ENFORCED RULES IN BASEBALL, #1

3.09. Players of opposing teams shall not fraternize at any time while in uniform.

The rules for substitution are laid out here. Once a player is removed from a game and replaced with a substitute, he can't go back in—and the substitute has to bat in the same position in the batting order as the player he's substituting for. If two or more players enter the game, the manager has to tell the umpire which player is batting where in the order. Managers in the National League, where the pitcher still has to come to bat, often use the *double switch*—when calling for a pitcher, they substitute for another player as well, someone who is coming to bat soon, and for whom the substitute can, essentially, pinch-hit. For example, the pitcher usually bats ninth. But if you take the pitcher and another player out at the same time— say, the player batting sixth—you can put the pitcher in the sixth spot in the order, and the new guy in the ninth spot. If the leadoff batter in the next inning is the ninth batter, you get a hitter in the leadoff spot, and the pitcher doesn't have to come up until much later.

A substitute is considered to have entered the game if, as a pitcher, he takes his place on the pitcher's plate, or as a batter in the batter's box, or as a fielder when play commences, or as a runner when he gets to the base. This rule ensured what must be the shortest career in Major League Baseball. Everyone who read W. P. Kinsella's *Shoeless Joe*, or saw the movie they made from it, *Field of Dreams*, knows about Moonlight Graham and his one-half-inning major league career; but compared to Larry Yount, Graham's career was lengthy. Yount was a pitcher for Houston, brought up for his debut in September, 1971. He was announced, came to the mound, took his warm-up pitches, pulled a muscle so he couldn't throw anymore, and was promptly replaced with another pitcher. He never threw a pitch, never fielded a ball or swung a bat, never did anything except warm up and hurt himself; and he was never seen in the big leagues again. But he officially appeared in a game and is duly listed in *The Baseball Encyclopedia* as having been a major league ballplayer.

Although umpires have the responsibility for stopping play when rain or some other condition makes play impossible, it's actually the home team's manager who has the responsibility for starting the game in the first place. If he doesn't think the field is fit, he can refuse to start the game. When he hands his lineup card to the umpire-in-chief (in duplicate, by the way, one copy of which is returned to him by the umpire), then the game has officially begun, and all decisions about it continuing or stopping rest with the umpire. Once the lineup card is given to the umpire, you can't change the order in which players bat for the rest of the game.

> *"You can't sit on a lead and run a few plays into the line and just kill the clock. You've got to throw the ball over the goddam plate and give the other man his chance. That's why baseball is the greatest game of them all."*
> —EARL WEAVER

A regulation game is nine innings long. The visiting team bats at the top of each inning; the home team comes to the plate at the bottom of all nine. If the score is tied at the end of nine innings, the game keeps going until someone wins. If the visiting team scores first in extra innings, the game is not over until the home team has its chance at bat, wherein it can tie or win the game. If a game is called because of weather or any other reason, it's an "official game" if five or more innings have been played. If a game is called in the middle of an inning after five innings have been played, it becomes a suspended game if (1) the visiting team has scored one or more runs to tie the score, and the home team has not scored, or (2) the visiting team has scored one or more runs to take the lead, and the home team has not tied the score or retaken the lead. Suspended games must be replayed from the point of suspension, with the same lineup as if the game had never stopped. If the score is tied when the game is called at the end of an inning, it must be replayed from the beginning.

LIVE BALLS AND DEAD

When the umpire calls "Play" (in The Book, umpires always call— they never yell, shout, or even raise their voices), the game begins and the ball is live until such time as the umpire calls "Time," at which point the ball becomes dead. In practice, you'll notice that often umpires call nothing at all when they want play to begin— they simply wait until the right moment and then point at the pitcher, indicating it's time to get going.

Nothing can happen while the ball is dead except that runners can advance one or more bases because of something that happened before the ball was declared dead. Among those events is a batter being hit by a pitched ball. In such a case, the ball is dead; the batter goes to first; and any runners on base who are forced advance one base. (In other words, if a man is already on first, he goes to second. If there's only one man on second, he stays where he is.) The ball is also dead when a balk is committed (see Chapter 3), and it's dead if a foul ball is hit and not caught on a fly. In the latter case, the umpire cannot call "Play" until all runners have returned to touch their bases.

Contrary to the belief of certain managers, coaches, and players, starting an argument with an umpire does not make the ball dead. Some players have learned this the hard way. David Cone, when he was pitching for the Mets in 1990 in a game against Atlanta, got involved in a long dispute with the first base umpire over whether he had touched first base in trying to put out a runner.

While he talked, Atlanta scored two runs, despite second baseman Gregg Jefferies' impassioned pleas to his pitcher to stop arguing and throw the ball. The Mets lost the game, 7–4.

Earl Weaver, manager of the Baltimore Orioles, violating Rule 9.02(a). Weaver has even managed to bump into the umpire, Marty Springstead, and give new meaning to the phrase "to flip one's lid." Weaver was, of course, ejected. To add insult to injury, the White Sox beat the Orioles 4–3.   *Associated Press*

> LEAST-OFTEN ENFORCED RULES IN BASEBALL, #2
>
> *4.06(a)(2). No manager, player, substitute, coach, trainer, or batboy shall at any time, whether from the bench, the coach's box, or on the playing field or elsewhere, use language which will in any manner refer to or reflect upon opposing players, an umpire, or any spectator.*

There are special rules for batted balls that hit umpires. If the umpire at the plate gets in the way of the catcher trying to make a throw, the ball is dead, and the runners can't advance. If a fair ball touches an umpire after it has passed the pitcher and it isn't caught by an outfielder, it's a dead ball. On the other hand, if a fair ball touches an umpire while still in flight and then is caught by an infielder, it's not an out, and the ball is in play—the umpire becomes, essentially, a part of the field. He's part of the field on a passed ball or wild pitch, too—if the ball hits him, it's just as if it hit the ground, and it's still in play.

UP AT BAT

Many Little Leaguers (and maybe even some beyond that level) think that if you step out of the batter's box, time is automatically called. Not so. You have to ask the umpire for time-out, and stepping out of the batter's box after the pitcher comes to a set position means nothing—the pitcher should go right ahead and pitch, and the umpire will call a ball or strike as appropriate, no matter where the batter is standing. In fact, once the pitcher has started a windup or come to the set position, even asking for time won't get you anywhere. The Book is very specific on this point—the batter can't ask for time even if he has "steamed glasses," or "dust in his eyes." The Book actually puts these things in quotation marks just to show exactly how lame it considers such excuses.

The batter is supposed to stay inside one of the two batter's boxes, 4' × 3' rectangles, one on each side of the plate, laid out in chalk on the ground before every game. As the game progresses, the lines start to disappear, but every umpire knows where they are, even if he can't see them after the third inning. If the batter doesn't stand inside this box, the umpire can, theoretically, tell the pitcher to pitch and call a strike each time. In practice, they rarely do this. Occasionally, you'll see an umpire remind a particularly egregious offender of where he is supposed to stand by borrowing his bat and elaborately drawing a line in the dirt.

Most of the time, batters make an out. This is partly because there are so many ways to do so. If you hit a fly ball that is caught, you're out. If you hit a ground ball and the fielder throws to first before you get there, you're out. If you get three strikes, you're out. If you foul tip a ball with two strikes and the catcher holds on to it, you're out. If you bunt foul with two strikes, you're out. If you hit the ball and it bounces up and hits you while you're not in the batter's box, you're out. If your bat hits the ball twice, you're out. If you run out of the baseline to avoid a tag, you're out. You're out if you hit a ball when you're not inside the batter's box; you're out if you pass the runner in front of you on the base paths; you're out if you step from one batter's box to the other while the pitcher is in the set position; you're out if you interfere with the catcher's throw by stepping out of the batter's box; and you're out if you bat out of turn.

If a batter bats out of turn, anyone on the field (or in the stands, for that matter) can shout about it, but the umpire can't. That's because batting out of turn is an *appeal play*, one of several The Book provides for. Someone has to appeal to the umpire to have the rule enforced—otherwise, it won't be. There's a specific reason for this, too, and The Book states it: "This rule is designed to require constant vigilance by the players and managers of both teams." Sitting on the bench during a baseball game is not meant to be a good opportunity for a nap. You wouldn't think batting out of turn would happen much in the majors, but they nod off from time to time even in the Show.

When we were kids, a demonstrated understanding of the infield fly rule was the true test of whether you knew baseball. This may or may not still be true, but even if it isn't, you should know the rule and why it exists. It only comes into effect when there are less than two out with men on first and second or the bases loaded. If a batter hits a pop fly in fair territory to the infield under these circumstances, he's automatically out, regardless of whether the fielder catches it. This is to prevent the fielder from intentionally dropping the ball and then starting a double play. A foul pop-up cannot be an infield fly because a dropped one would just be a foul ball and couldn't be the start of a double play. It's important to remember that this rule doesn't apply to line drives or popped-up bunts, which a fielder can legally drop or trap intentionally. The reasoning here is that liners and bunts can be difficult to catch on a fly, unlike ordinary pop-ups. So a fielder shouldn't be penalized for failing to catch one—deliberately or not—and then going for the double play.

LEAST-OFTEN ENFORCED RULES IN BASEBALL, #3

9.02(a). Any umpire's decision which involves judgment, such as, but not limited to, whether a batted ball is fair or foul, whether a pitch is a strike or a ball, or whether a runner is safe or out, is final. No player, manager, coach, or substitute shall object to any such judgment decisions.

Sometimes, of course, batters don't make out. Four balls, and you go to first "without liability to be put out," as The Book puts it. If you're hit by a pitch, you go to first—but you have to have made an attempt to get out of the way. You can't just stand there and "take one for the team," even though such altruism is much admired. Also, if the ball is in the strike zone when it hits you, it's a strike, and you don't go anywhere—you just feel pain. You can run to first on a third strike if the catcher drops or misses the ball, but you're subject to being put out in the usual ways, by tagging or by a throw that beats you to first base. You can only run on a dropped third strike when there is no one on first or when there's a man on first with two out.

You're safe at first if you hit a runner with your batted ball (although the runner is out). If a fair ball touches an umpire in fair territory before touching or passing a fielder, you're safe at first. If a player deflects your hit into the stands, you get a double. And of course if you hit a ball out of the park in fair territory, it's a home run and you get to "touch 'em all."

ON THE BASE PATHS

A runner is entitled to a base when he touches it before he's out, and he can stay there until he's forced to move because another runner is following him (or because there are three out and it's his turn to play the field). If he wants to advance, he has to touch all the bases in order—and if he has to return for any reason, he has to touch the bases in reverse order. No shortcuts are allowed.

"No two men on a base," as we all know, but you have to tag the interloper—the following runner—for him to be out. Otherwise, he's free to correct the situation himself by running back to the previous base (or by having the preceding runner head for the next base). It rarely happens that runners wind up in this predicament, but when it does, you'll usually see the fielder tag everyone in sight, including the umpire and any coaches within reach, just to make sure. There's even one true story of three men who wound up on third base at the same time—the 1926 Brooklyn Dodgers were famous for such plays. It happened in a game against the Boston Braves (yes, the same Braves who later moved to Milwaukee and then to Atlanta, where Ted Turner bought the team). Seems the bases were loaded with one out: Chick Fewster on first, the legendary Dazzy Vance on second, and Hank DeBerry on third. Babe Herman came up to bat and hit a shot off the center field wall. Hank DeBerry immediately scored, preserving his dignity. Fewster took off from first and was already on his way to third when Vance got hung up between third and home. Herman, eyes fixed firmly on the ground in front of him, was by now chugging along right behind Fewster. The third base coach, Mickey O'Neil, who was actually a second-string catcher coaching third for the first and only time in his life, saw the disaster developing and started yelling, "Back! Back!"—to Herman, that is, who was about to run right over Fewster. But Vance, a pitcher whose lifetime .150 batting average suggests a possible lack of baserunning experience, assumed that he was the object of the yelling, so he headed back to third. By this time, Fewster was standing idly on third base, where he was in a perfect position to watch Herman slide into third from one side and Vance from the other. Eddie Taylor, who was the Boston third baseman, proceeded to tag first Vance and then Herman. Why he didn't also tag Fewster is one of history's great unanswered questions. Fewster was some-one who apparently couldn't leave bad enough alone: He assumed that because both his companions had been tagged, that was three out. Wrong! Only Herman was out—third base belonged to Vance, and he was touching it, so tagging him meant nothing. Taylor would have had to tag Fewster to make the third out. Fewster, untouched and still unknowing, now trotted over to take his defensive position at second base. Boston's second baseman, Doc Gautreau, one of the few people in the infield who still had his wits about him, called for the ball. Fewster finally caught on and tried to escape, but Gautreau ran him down and tagged him for the final out of the inning.

LEAST-OFTEN ENFORCED RULES IN BASEBALL, #4

Rule 7.06(b).(Note): The catcher, without the ball in his possession, has no right to block the pathway of the runner attempting to score. The base belongs to the runner, and the catcher should be there only when he is fielding a ball or when he already has the ball in his hand.

Every runner except the batter can move to the next base without anyone being able to put him out when the pitcher balks, when he's forced by a batter who is entitled to his base (because of a walk, balk, or interference), or when a batted ball hits another runner or an umpire before it has passed or been touched by a fielder. You've seen the spectacular play when a fielder dives into the crowd to make a catch. If he succeeds in catching the ball, good for him. The batter is out. But the downside is that the runner or runners on base get to advance one base for free. If it's a foul ball, in other words, and there's a man on third with less than two out, he'd be better off not catching it at all than catching it and then tumbling into someone's lap.

If fielders try to stop a batted or thrown ball by throwing their gloves, hats, or catcher's masks at it, the penalties are severe. You'll rarely see it happen in the major leagues—it isn't the sort of thing you'd do by accident—but if anyone dared throw his glove at a batted ball, the batter would be entitled to three bases for free, and so would all the runners. Throwing your glove at a thrown ball gives the batter and runners two bases for free.

A runner is out, of course, if a fielder tags him with the ball when he's not standing on a base. The only exception is first base, which you're allowed to run past as long as you go straight back to the base. Returning directly is the key here—if you make an attempt to go to second you are, as The Book always says, "liable to be put out."

And a runner is also out if he fails to tag up—touch his base—after a fly ball (fair or foul) is caught and before he or the base is touched by the fielder with the ball in hand. Failing to tag up is another appeal play—the umpire won't call it unless someone on the defensive team asks him to.

If a runner interferes with a fielder, he's out. Sometimes interference is obvious: If, for example, a batter hits a fair ball and then hits it again with his bat, that's clearly interference. Same call if he deliberately tries to deflect the course of a batted ball with his hands or feet (or if he blows on it—yes, it has been tried). But more often, the call involves making a judgment in an ambiguous situation. When a runner slides into second base to try to break up a double play, how enthusiastic can his efforts be before they're declared interference? This is a particularly controversial call, because if there's interference here, it's an automatic double play. A third base coach, for another example, could be called for interference if he makes motions while a man is on third that imitate a runner heading for home. So how good an imitation does it have to be? If a runner deliberately bumps into a fielder fielding a ball, that's interference—but who can tell what's deliberate?

As you can imagine, interference calls have caused plenty of arguments, some so famous and so crucial to the outcome of important games that they're still being debated years later in ballparks and bars all over the country.

Picture this: Boston Red Sox and Cincinnati Reds. Third game of the 1975 World Series. Score tied 5–5, bottom of the tenth inning, nobody out. Cesar Geronimo on first; Ed Armbrister at bat. Armbrister bunts, slapping the ball into the artificial turf. The ball bounces up, and Carlton Fisk, the Boston catcher, goes after it. Armbrister tangles himself up with Fisk; Fisk untangles himself, grabs the ball, and throws wildly over second base into center field. The runners make it to second and third; Fisk looks for the interference call, but umpire Larry Barnett says nothing. Three plays later, the Red Sox lose the game.

The videotape of the play clearly showed interference, but Barnett argued that there could be no interference unless it was "deliberate." And he found some support in the rules. Rule 7.09(h) does use the words "willfully and deliberately" to qualify "interfering," but the rule only discusses interfering with a double play. In any case, the rule has now been changed: Today, if a runner interferes with a fielder trying to make a play—deliberately or otherwise—he's out, and no runners can advance. This rule change has done nothing to alleviate the chronic pain of Red Sox fans.

ETIQUETTE TIPS FOR PITCHERS

Pitchers are very restricted in the kinds of motions they can make. When men are on base, they operate under particularly severe constraints. If they stand wrong, or move their hands incorrectly, or throw to a base in the wrong way, or even accidentally drop the ball while they're standing on the pitcher's rubber, they're guilty. The penalty is a balk, and a balk means all runners advance a base.

LEAST-OFTEN ENFORCED RULES IN BASEBALL, #5

8.02(a)1–6. The pitcher shall not (1) bring his pitching hand in contact with his mouth or lips while in the 18-foot circle surrounding the pitching rubber . . . ; (2)apply a foreign substance of any kind to the ball; (3) expectorate on the ball, either hand or his glove; (4) rub the ball on his glove, person, or clothing; (5) deface the ball in any manner; (6) deliver what is called the "shine" ball, "spit" ball, "mud" ball, or "emery" ball.

It is notoriously difficult for fans to spot a balk. Usually, nothing seems to be happening when suddenly one or more umpires starts shouting, and a runner advances. The spectators, even the ones who get to see the replay on TV, are perplexed. The ones in the stadium just have to accept the call. Actually, the rule itself isn't so hard. For the record, Rule 8.05 says that the pitcher has balked if he does any of the following:

• Moves as if to pitch, but then doesn't

• While touching the pitcher's rubber, fakes a throw to first base

• While touching the rubber, fails to step directly toward the base he is throwing to

- Throws, or fakes a throw, to an unoccupied base, except when making a play

- Pitches when he isn't facing the batter, or when the batter isn't ready

- Makes pitching motions while not touching the rubber

- Unnecessarily delays the game

- Stands on or astride the rubber without the ball in hand

- After coming to a legal pitching position, removes his hand from the ball, or drops it intentionally or otherwise

- Pitches when the catcher is not in the catcher's box

- Delivers the pitch from the set position without coming to a stop

If you can spot a balk and call it just before the umpires do, the fans around you will stare in wide-eyed amazement, waiting for the next piece of wisdom to fall from your lips. My advice is this: Shout "Balk" often, even if you're not quite sure. You'll usually be wrong—so just complain about the umpire's eyesight. Then one day you'll be right, and your reputation as an expert will be assured.

LEAST-OFTEN ENFORCED RULES IN BASEBALL, #6

8.04. When bases are unoccupied, the pitcher shall deliver the ball to the batter within 20 seconds after he receives the ball. Each time the pitcher delays the game by violating this rule, the umpire shall call "Ball."

Pitching inside is essential, but beanballs are not allowed. (See Chapter 3 for an explanation of the subtle differences between various kinds of inside pitches.) If a pitcher does intentionally throw at a batter—and it is up to the umpire to decide if that's what happened—the umpire can toss the offender out of the game. He can also throw the manager out. Or he can warn the pitcher and manager of both teams that the next time a pitcher on either team does it, that pitcher and his manager are going to be escorted off the field. What's more, the umpire can officially warn both teams even before play begins, which he will do if there is reason to expect bad blood between the two teams. The Book is pretty firm about all this, and to make its view of the matter perfectly clear, it adds, "To pitch at a batter's head is unsportsmanlike and highly dangerous. It should be—and is—condemned by everybody."

When a pitcher goes to the mound to start a new inning, or when a new pitcher comes into a game, he gets to warm up by throwing exactly eight pitches before the batter takes his place in the batter's box. If a pitcher is brought in because of a sudden emergency—an injury, usually—he can have extra time to warm up at the discretion of the umpire.

Everyone has seen the manager come out and talk to the pitcher. He's allowed to do this twice in an inning (though not while the same batter is up), but the second time he comes out, the pitcher has to be replaced. Some managers used to try to evade this rule by talking to a catcher or another player, and then having that player visit the mound. No dice, says The Book. If you do that, it's a trip to the mound just like any other.

TRUTH AND JUSTICE

Although The Book only specifies that "one or more" be present, most major league games have four umpires officiating—one for each base and one to call balls and strikes at home plate. In All-Star games, playoffs, and World Series games, the custom has been to have six umpires—in addition to the original four, one is stationed on each foul line in the outfield.

Arguing with the umpire is so much a part of baseball that it's hard to believe that The Book actually prohibits most arguments. But if you say, as The Book does, that you're not allowed to argue about anything that involves "judgment" on the part of the umpire, well, that doesn't leave much to argue about. The fact is that managers, players, and coaches argue about "judgment" all the time; and unless they argue too vociferously or use certain key words guaranteed to get them thrown off the field (we don't have to list them—let's just say that one of the words is "bush," and a lot of the others have four letters, too), they usually are allowed to say their piece and then go on with the game. The one place where the "judgment" rule is usually enforced is concerning balls and strikes. If a manager or player argues with the umpire about that, he's very likely to be invited to leave. There is one near-exception: If there's a half swing that the umpire calls a ball, the catcher or the manager may ask the plate umpire to get help from the first or third base umpire to verify the checked swing. Even here, though, you're not allowed to complain that the call was improper—only that the umpire didn't ask for help. Of course, managers have their ways of arguing balls and strikes without actually mentioning balls and strikes—it's just amazing how many euphemisms you can come up with to substitute for those terms. Some umpires are more tolerant of such ploys than others.

The Book does permit discussions of rule interpretation. If there is a reasonable doubt, a manager may appeal a decision, provided he makes that appeal only to the umpire who made the decision in the first place—you're not allowed to go from one umpire to another trying to find a sympathetic ear. Umpires may ask another umpire for advice—though the rules help preserve the dignity of the profession of umpiring by prohibiting one umpire from offering advice to another without being asked.

The Book, while clearly recognizing that the task of an umpire is difficult and often thankless, nevertheless makes strong appeals to duty, conscience, and character: "It is often a trying position," it says, "which requires the exercise of much patience and good judgment, but do not forget that the first essential in working out of a bad situation is to keep your own temper and self-control." And finally, "But remember! The first requisite is to get decisions correctly."

KEEPING SCORE

Perhaps more than most team sports, baseball is a game of records. Almost everything you do in a baseball game can be measured and then recorded. Success and failure can be and are delineated in stark numbers. A baseball player's competency is public knowledge— there's his batting average, his earned run average, his on-base percentage, everything right out there where everyone can see it. Most of us at least get the privilege of a "confidential employee evaluation" or some such thing, but a ballplayer's evaluation is as public as tomorrow morning's newspaper. We'll have more to say about records and statistics in Chapter 4; but we can't entirely ignore the subject here because scoring—who gets a hit, who doesn't—is part of the *Official Baseball Rules,* and The Book offers all the details.

Every game has an Official Scorer—the person who decides whether a batter got on because of a hit or an error. There aren't really any "professional" baseball scorers. The people assigned the task— appointed by the league's president—are usually sportswriters.

He has to do quite a bit of writing during the game. The Book specifies at least twenty different things that can happen at bat and have to be written down, a half dozen things a fielder must have records for, and more than twenty-five pitching events, all of which have to be noted in the Official Scorer's report on the game. Then he has to become an accountant to "prove" his box score. In other words, he has to make sure that the number of at bats, walks, hit batters, sacrifices, and batters given first base because of interference is exactly the same as the total of runs, players left on base, and opposing team's putouts.

Probably the most important part of his job—at least the part that attracts the most attention—is deciding what's a hit and what's an error. Making a mistake here risks angering any number of people—the batter, the pitcher, and the fans, not to mention the player's agent, who may be negotiating next year's contract. Fair balls that allow a player to make it to first are hits, but you don't get a hit if you force a preceding runner out at another base. That's a fielder's choice, and it counts as a time at bat without being a hit. Sometimes even if the preceding runner isn't put out, you still won't get a hit if, in the scorer's judgment, you should have been put out with ordinary effort on the part of the fielder. You get a hit if your ball takes a bad bounce; but you don't get a hit if the ball goes through the fielder's legs or he otherwise botches the play. That's an error, and it decreases your batting average.

The rules for RBIs—runs batted in—are a little different. You can be credited with an RBI even if you hit into a fielder's choice. No hit, but you do get the ribbie. If you hit into a double play and a run scores, however, you get neither the hit nor the RBI. And you don't get an RBI if the run scored because of an error. A sacrifice that scores a run is an RBI, and if you walk with the bases full, you get the RBI in addition to the walk (and no time at bat counted).

The scorer decides if hits are singles, doubles, or triples. If you make it to second base, it isn't necessarily a double: If a man is thrown out at third on the play, then it's only a single. Same principle applies to triples: If a man is thrown out at home, you only get a double, even if you're standing there safe at third. Also, you can be thrown out at second or third and still get credit for a single or a double, despite your bad judgment about trying to take that extra base.

Even a stolen base isn't always a stolen base. If there's an error that prevents a runner from being tagged out, he gets credited with a "caught stealing" even if he wasn't actually caught. And if the opposing team doesn't even try to get him out, he won't get credited with a stolen base either. It has to be earned. On a double steal, you don't get credit for a steal if the other runner is put out, even though you're safe.

A sacrifice bunt is a sacrifice and not a time at bat if it advances a runner. But a sacrifice fly is not a sacrifice unless it advances the runner all the way home to score.

Fielders get credit for putouts when they catch a fly (fair or foul), catch a thrown ball that puts out a runner (the catcher is the beneficiary of this rule when a batter strikes out), or tag a runner. In addition, there is a long list of automatic putouts credited to the catcher—when a batter is called out for batting out of turn, for instance, the catcher gets an automatic putout. Other fielders can get automatic putouts, too. For example, if a runner passes the runner in front of him, he's out, and the putout goes to the fielder nearest the point of the offense. For every out, someone must be credited with a putout. All accounts must balance.

Fortunately for the rest of us, our errors are neither so clearly defined nor so conscientiously recorded as those of professional baseball players. For these people, every misplay, bobble, fumble, botch, and bungle is noticed and carefully written down. An error is any mistake that prolongs a batter's time at the plate or a runner's life on the bases beyond what would otherwise be its normal duration. A player doesn't even have to touch a ball to be given an error—if it goes through his legs, he'll get the error regardless of whether he touched it. On the other hand, if he chases a ball but doesn't get to it in time, even though it may seem he should have, he'll rarely be given an error. Mental mistakes—throwing to the wrong base, failing to get the lead runner, and so on—are just mistakes, not errors. Fielders can make errors on throws, too, and if the throw allowed a runner to advance a base, they'll get an error even if the throw took a bad hop or touched an umpire or did something else seemingly out of the control of the thrower. Every base advanced, as The Book says, has to be somehow accounted for, however unjust this may sometimes seem.

A pitcher counts his career in earned runs—runs that are not the result of errors, but of the pitcher's giving up hits or walks (including intentional walks, by the way). To be fair to pitchers, if a batter gets on base because of an error, interference, or on a hit after his turn at bat was prolonged by someone dropping an easy foul pop-up, for example, then any run he scores will not be earned and will not go against the pitcher's earned run average. (See Chapter 4 for an illuminating discussion of earned run averages.) Relief pitchers are protected, too. If there were men on base when the relief pitcher came into the game and those men score, those runs, if earned, get charged to the pitcher who let those men get on base. If a relief pitcher comes in while a batter has an advantage in the count and that batter walks and then scores, the run will be charged to the starting pitcher, not the reliever. How much of an advantage? The Book is quite specific: The count must be 2–0, 2–1, 3–0, 3–1, or 3–2. If he gets on any other way except a walk, however, the run is charged to the relief pitcher. Just details? Maybe. But rather significant when it comes time to make next year's salary demands.

Pitchers not only have earned run averages, but also won-lost records, and there are rules for determining which pitcher gets credit for a win or a loss. If you pitch a complete game and your team wins, then it's pretty clear that you get the win. If you pitch five innings or more and your team is ahead when you leave and wins the game, you get the win. But pitchers don't always pitch five innings, much less a complete game. So there are somewhat involved ways of deciding who gets the credit for a win and who gets the blame for a loss. Sometimes it is left to the Official Scorer to decide which pitcher has been "most effective" in producing the win (it need not be the starter). The Book's syntax gets a little tortuous when trying to describe the techniques for making this decision; but in general, if your team pulled ahead while you were pitching and stays ahead after you leave, you'll usually get the win. Pinning a loss on someone is easier—if you're the first pitcher to be replaced when your team is behind and your team never regains the lead, you're the loser.

With the growing importance of relief pitchers, a relatively new category has been invented: the save. The term was first used to describe the work of the Brooklyn Dodgers' bullpen in the 1950s, but The Book didn't require records of saves to be kept until 1969. In any case, determining if a pitcher gets a save is relatively simple:

First, he has to be the finishing pitcher in a victory. Second, he cannot be the winning pitcher. And third, he must either enter the game with a lead of three runs or less and pitch for at least one inning; or enter the game with the potential tying run either on base, at bat, or in the on-deck circle; or simply pitch effectively for three innings.

That's a quick tour of the rule book. Now let's play some ball.

2

Playing the Field

Almost all Major League Baseball players have played baseball since they were kids. By the time a major league team expresses any interest in them, they've been playing the game for at least fifteen years. They've played in hundreds of games, perhaps thousands if you count the informal games they've been involved in, and they've watched many more. They've played for a Little League or Babe Ruth or American Legion team. They've played in high school. Many have played in college. Some have played in semi-pro leagues. They're all excellent athletes, often stars in other sports in addition to baseball. They're young and strong and fast. But few of them are ready for the majors. Basketball and football players can play right out of college; in fact, some don't even finish college before they undertake a pro career. But baseball almost always requires several years of minor league experience before a player is ready for the big leagues. Why?

Part of the explanation lies in the complexity and subtlety of the physical skills involved. Even the best players will stare and flail at many major league fastballs before they ever succeed in hitting one. The world's greatest athletes—Michael Jordan, for example—can be made to look clumsy and foolish by even a good minor league curveball. Turning a double play with major league hitters and runners or stealing a base on a major league pitcher and catcher is unlikely to be accomplished on the first try. But still more is required, something in addition to formidable physical skills: an understanding of strategy and tactics and the ability to apply the strategy instinctively while at the same time executing some of the most difficult physical maneuvers in all of sports. This is what takes so much time and so much practice to learn.

Baseball is by design a game that demands constant attention from all players—even while they seem to be doing nothing but sitting on the bench waiting for their turn at bat. If attention flags, even for a moment, failure is inevitable. Learning and mastering complex rules, understanding elaborate strategies, concentrating intensely, planning for every contingency—these are in most human endeavors marks of maturity, perhaps even wisdom. And they are all required to play baseball successfully. Strength, coordination, speed, and endurance are necessary—but not sufficient.

A player has to learn complex moves so thoroughly that they become instinctive. Man on first base, one out, left-handed hitter up, 3 and 1 count. You're playing shortstop. What's likely to happen with this particular hitter in this situation if the pitcher throws a high inside fastball? How do you even know he's throwing a fastball? What are you supposed to do when the ball is hit to you on the ground? On a pop-up? On a line drive? Over your head to the left fielder? Is the guy on first likely to steal on a 3 and 1 count? Should you be covering second? When the pitch is made and the ball is hit, a baseball player has to have all this and more in his brain—in his unconscious mind, you might even say—in order to do his job. The attentive fan has his head in the game too, and he's thinking (and guessing) along with the manager and all the players on the field.

PLAYING WITHOUT THE BALL

Although there are vast differences in the responsibilities of each of the players on the field, baseball is nevertheless a team sport in which all the separate pieces must come together to win ball games. We'll discuss each position in detail later in this chapter, but first let's see what the fielders are supposed to be doing when a batter swings and hits a ball at them.

> *"You can observe a lot just by watching."*
> —YOGI BERRA

Every defensive player has a job to do on every play, and the job varies depending on the game situation. When a ball is hit—no matter how many are out or who's on base—Every fielder moves. This ballet happens whenever a batter hits a fair ball: Every player is anticipating the hundreds of possible outcomes when a ball is put in play and moving himself to the best position to make putouts and prevent the opposing team from scoring runs. Everyone has a defensive assignment on every play, and, as coaches like to say, there's no defensive assignment called "stand there and stare."

Obviously, if there's no one out and someone hits a hard line drive to the shortstop, there's little for anyone to do; the play is over before anyone can do anything, and if the shortstop is skillful or lucky (or both) there's nothing left to do but throw the ball around the horn. Same goes for a routine grounder. But when someone gets a hit, it's time for damage control, and every player has to help.

Let's start with a simple situation. The bases are empty. The batter hits a single to left field. What's a fielder to do? There are some variations, depending on a manager's taste, but here's the way most managers would want their players to react. The second baseman covers second—that's where the throw is going to be coming in. The pitcher positions himself to back up the second baseman for that throw. The catcher stands up and runs toward first base—just in case there's a play on the runner there. The first baseman has two jobs: First, he has to make sure that the runner touches first base. Then he backs up second for added protection. The right fielder moves toward the infield—the left fielder might make a really wild throw, and he can back that up if the pitcher and the first baseman can't get to it. The center fielder runs over to back up the left fielder. The shortstop first tries to field the ball, and then when he decides he can't, he lines up between the left fielder and the second baseman to act as the relay, or cutoff man. The third baseman covers third. And that's about it. Oh yeah, the left fielder— the center of attention for most fans on a play like this—he picks up

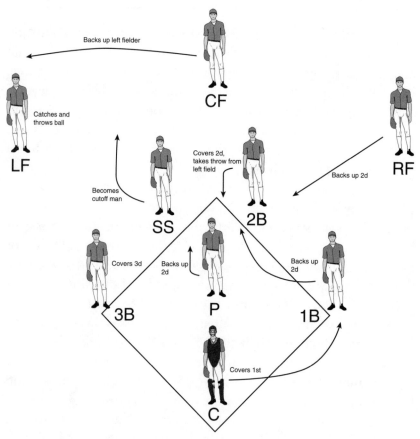

Bases empty; single to left field.

the ball and throws it, either to the shortstop (if he's in the proper cutoff position) or directly to second base (if the runner is heading there to try to stretch his single to a double). This is what happens on an ordinary single with no one on. With men on base, things can get complicated.

> *"They watch the ball game as if it were a hockey game. They wait for something to happen and then they cheer."*
> —KEN SINGLETON, LAMENTING THE LACK OF BASEBALL SAVVY OF MONTREAL EXPOS FANS.

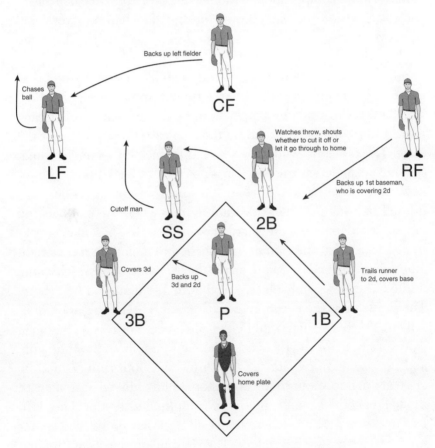

Man on first; one out. Double up left field line. Could be a triple.

Fielders are always anticipating something—anything and every-thing, in fact. And the fan is, too. Some sports provide constant scoring—basketball, for example. When Ken Singleton bemoaned the Montreal fans' ignorance, he was saying that fans should be on the edge of their seats cheering when they are *anticipating* something will happen—not just when it actually occurs. Watching baseball intelligently is anticipating every possibility, on offense or defense, good or bad, interesting or routine, conventionally exciting or not. That's what players and managers have to do, and fans should do it, too.

So let's take a situation that presents more possibilities for the defense, more complications to anticipate, more possible damage to control. Say there's a man on first, one out. The batter drives a ball right over third base, just fair when it hits 20 feet up the line from the base. In other words, a certain double that could easily turn into a triple. The left fielder, of course, takes off like a shot, trying to get to the ball fast enough to prevent the runner from scoring from first. What are his teammates supposed to be doing? The catcher can't move from home—he has to be there in case there's a play at the plate. The pitcher—who knows he has to back up second if some-one hits a single with no one on—now has to back up two bases, because he doesn't know where the throw is going. So he posts himself halfway between third and home, where he can back up either base depending on what happens. The first baseman checks to make sure that the runner has touched first, and then runs right after him to second, trying to arrive there simultaneously with him, in the (admittedly unlikely) event that there's a play on him there. The shortstop is the cutoff man on this play. He has to station him-self on a line between the left fielder and home. The second baseman leaves his base for the first baseman to cover, follows the shortstop, and stands where he can see the throw and both runners and be close enough to shout to the shortstop, telling him what to do with the ball once he catches the throw from the left fielder. The third baseman covers third—there may well be a play there. The center fielder backs up the left fielder. The right fielder backs up the first baseman, who is now covering second. And you thought these guys were just standing around spitting!

> *"When one of them guys hits a single to you, throw the ball to third. That way we can hold them to a double."*
> —CASEY STENGEL, ADDRESSING THE PITIABLE OUTFIELD OF THE 1962 N.Y. METS

By this time, the left fielder has fielded the ball, and now he has to decide where to throw it. He wants to prevent the run from scoring; but if he can't do that, he certainly doesn't want to let the runner turn a double into a triple. This is where one of the "fundamentals" that managers are always talking about comes into play: "Always hit the cutoff man." The left fielder wants to throw the ball in such a way that, left untouched, it will go straight to the catcher to prevent the run from scoring. But he also has to throw it so that it can be cut off by the shortstop in case it's too late to prevent the run. The second baseman directs traffic. If he thinks there's a play at the plate, he'll yell to the shortstop to let the ball go through. If not, he'll tell him to cut it off and nail the runner trying to make it to third— or direct the throw back to second if he sees a play there. A throw that goes over the shortstop's head and then arrives at the plate too late to get the runner will not only allow the run to score, but will also allow the trailing runner to make it to third. Bad play. Instead of one run in, two outs, and no one on, you've got one run in, one out, and a man on third.

Even if you don't get a man out at third this way, a good throw cut off by the shortstop will keep him at second. One out and a man on second is a much better state of affairs for the defense than one out and a man on third. Even though third is only twice as close to home as second, it's much easier to score from there. With one out, there are nine sure ways to score from third, none of which will work from second. A grounder to the infield will do it. A sacrifice fly.

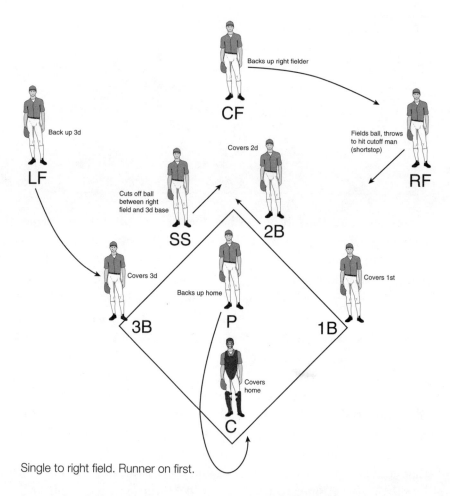

Single to right field. Runner on first.

A sacrifice bunt or a squeeze play. An error, of course, or any base hit, even a little blooper just past the second baseman. A wild pitch, a passed ball, or a balk will all score a run for you. The moral to this story is—as you've already guessed—"Always hit the cutoff man!"

What should a fan be watching in this situation? Yes, it's enough to make your head spin. Obviously, your eye is going to follow the hit down the third base line toward the left fielder. How deep is the left fielder playing, how fast does he get to the ball, and how good is his arm? Left field has traditionally been a place to stick good hitters who are poor fielders with weak arms. Luis Polonia, who plays left

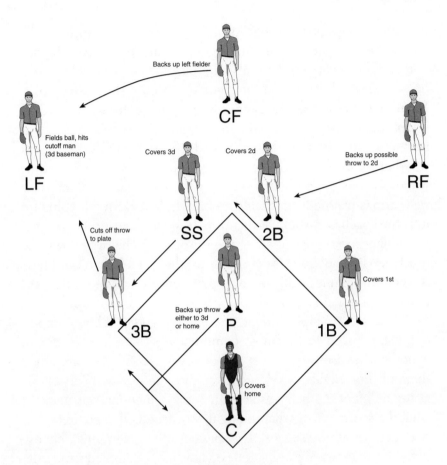

Single to left field. Runners on first and second.

for the Atlanta Braves, is an example. But today's left fielders—Polonia included—are usually speedsters who can get to the ball fast. Rickey Henderson, Bernard Gilkey, Barry Bonds, and Vince Coleman all have wheels. So you're watching someone fast get to the ball, but you're going to have to wonder in many cases whether the throw that follows will be good. So your eye should come down the left field line to the shortstop—the cutoff man. Where is he playing and will he be able to wheel and throw to the plate? While you're seeing where he's positioning himself, you still have to be watching the runner coming around from first, your eye measuring his progress against the progress of the left fielder in getting to the ball and throwing it. Will the runner round third and try to go home? You certainly don't want to miss the play at the plate—if there is one—and you'd like to see the run score even if there isn't a play. Figuring out whether this runner is going to try to score, it would seem, requires an expert's opinion. Fortunately, there is such an expert available: the third base coach. It's his job to tell the runner whether to head for home or hold up at third. So if you have time while all this is going on, it's interesting to steal a glance at him. If his right arm is windmilling around, get ready: The runner is going for it. If the coach is pushing his hands palms open toward the ground, he's telling the runner to slide into third. If he's halfway down the third base line holding his palms toward the runner, then third base is where the runner will stay, even if he rounds the base and seems to be headed home.

These two examples should give you some idea of how complex defense is, even in the most common of situations. These two hypothetical cases are simple to begin with, and we've simplified them further. In fact, we brought you into the situation very late— at the moment the ball was actually hit. No mention was made of what the score was or what inning it was, factors that could be important. Nor did we suggest what pitches the pitcher might choose in these situations. We didn't tell you how many balls and strikes the hitter had on him at the time. We offered no information about the particular skills or tendencies of the hitter, though all the fielders would know these and use them in their calculations about where to position themselves and what to expect. We didn't say, in the second example, whether the man on first was a threat to steal, or who would cover second if he did try to take a base. We never alluded to the possibility that the hitter might bunt, or what the fielders would do to prepare for that. We didn't even tell you if the hitter was left- or right-handed. Yet all these factors, and more, would be important. At all nine positions on the field, minds were working—even before the batter walked up to the plate—to figure out what might happen next and to figure out a way to be prepared for it. Let's take a look at each defensive position to try to understand what those players are thinking, and why.

PITCHING

This is where it all starts. Baseball, it is said, is the only game where the defense holds the ball, and the pitcher is the one who holds it first. Does good pitching beat good hitting, or is it the other way around? Depends on who you talk to (and sometimes on how loud you can argue). Hank Aaron, one of the greatest hitters of all time, once said, "I've got a bat. All the pitcher has is a ball. That gives me a natural advantage." Well, maybe in the case of Aaron, but even the best hitters only succeed about one-third of the time. The least that can be said about pitching is that it's hard to hit.

> *"Nothing flatters me more than to have it assumed that I could write prose—unless it be to have it assumed that I once pitched baseball with distinction."*
> —ROBERT FROST

Major league pitchers can throw a baseball with great accuracy at speeds above ninety miles per hour. To do this, they twist, turn, snap their wrists and elbows, push with their legs, and throw their entire bodies off the mound, twisting and leaping toward the plate. Pitching looks like it's hard on the body, and it is, especially so on the arm. Many pitchers have to wrap their elbows in ice after every game to keep the swelling down, and almost none of them can pitch more than once every four or five days. Teams have twenty-five players on a squad for most of the season, and on most teams, between nine and twelve of them are pitchers.

Righties and Lefties

> *"Left-handers have more enthusiasm for life. They sleep on the wrong side of the bed and their head gets more stagnant on that side."*
> —CASEY STENGEL

Although there may be individual exceptions, it is statistically clear that right-handed hitters find it easier to hit left-handed pitchers, and left-handed hitters find it easier to hit righties. Right-handed hitters say that they have an extra fraction of a second to pick up the ball when it's coming out of the pitcher's left hand, and left-handed hitters enjoy the same view when facing a right-handed pitcher— the ball comes from a place more central to the hitter's field of vision.

Even in the best hitters, this difference is clear. Lefty Wade Boggs, for example, hit .398 against righties in 1983, but .281 against lefties. Ted Williams, another left-handed hitter, hit a remarkable .396 against lefties in 1941—and a flabbergasting .461 against righties. A manager expends a good deal of effort during games trying to manipulate this statistical advantage—that is, trying to make the opposition's right-handed batters face his own team's right-handed pitchers, and their lefties face his left-handed pitchers.

Because most pitchers are right-handed (about 70 percent of them), you would think that this would put right-handed batters at a disadvantage. They ought to have lower batting averages, as a group, than lefties. They do. Statistician Pete Palmer figured out that between 1974 and 1978, righties hit about .261, and lefties about .281. That lefties have an extra step on righties in beating out infield hits is true, but it's hard to believe that this could be a major contributing factor since there aren't enough infield hits to make that much of a difference.

Why Pitchers Can't Hit

Some pitchers hit pretty well—a contemporary example is Orel Hershiser when he played with the Dodgers, and there are historical examples from Babe Ruth to Don Newcombe and many others. But with most pitchers, you're lucky if you can get them to properly lay down a bunt. How come?

The reason is that pitchers aren't selected for their hitting. All other players have to be able to hit to get to the majors, but pitching is such a specialized (and desirable) skill that pitchers can get there without being good hitters. And of course they don't have to be good hitters to stay in the majors, so they concentrate on the skills that got them there. In the National League, pitchers still have to come up to bat in their turn. In the American League, they've confirmed the status of pitchers by instituting the designated hitter—the player who bats in place of the pitcher, but doesn't play the field—so that American League pitchers never even get up to bat.

> *"I've changed my mind about it [the designated hitter]. Instead of being bad, it stinks."*
>
> —SPARKY ANDERSON

"Work Fast, Change Speeds, Throw Strikes"

This age-old admonition of pitching coaches to pitchers is both advice and encouragement. The best pitchers get a rhythm going: The pitches come quickly, one after the other. The best pitchers rely on fastballs, but they know that you have to keep batters off balance by changing speeds—throwing slower pitches in certain situations. And of course, the best pitchers are always ahead in the count—throwing strikes means that you avoid giving up walks, and always pitch with the batter at a disadvantage.

Balls and Strikes

The old joke has it that when a catcher and a manager go up to the pitcher's mound at a crucial point in the game for what looks like a long and involved discussion of intricate defensive plans and techniques, the only thing they actually tell him—and they tell him every time—is: "Throw strikes." Of course this isn't quite true—pitchers sometimes have to be reminded that a given runner might steal, that a certain game situation requires a certain pitch, that he got this batter out on a curveball in the dirt the last time he was up, and so on. But at the same time, there must be some truth in the story, because it is perfectly obvious that any defensive strategy, however subtle and complex, will work better if the pitcher puts the ball over the plate and the batter can't hit it.

Getting the first pitch to be a strike is particularly important, and there are statistics to prove it. Pete Palmer, coauthor of *The Hidden Game of Baseball*, did a study of more than 2,500 at bats during which the batting average was .259. When the pitcher got the first pitch in for a strike, the average declined to .240. When he didn't, it went up to .267. With an 0–2 count, the batters in Palmer's study hit an anemic .198. Some of the most intelligent baseball men are apparently unaware of how radical the change can be. Keith Hernandez, for example, in his book *Pure Baseball*, says Wade Boggs "isn't afraid to hit with two strikes on him." Well, maybe he isn't afraid, but Boggs, who has a lifetime batting average hovering around .335, hits .265 when he's 0–2. For a pitcher, it's like magic: If you want to turn Wade Boggs into a .265 hitter, just get two strikes on him. On the average, a .300 hitter will hit about 100 points higher when he's ahead in the count than when he's behind.

The rules define the strike zone as the space over home plate and between the armpits and the knees of the batter in his natural stance. Home plate is 17 inches wide. The average ballplayer is, say, 6 feet tall, and his strike zone will be about 2 feet high. So the strike zone is a rectangle in the air, the bottom of it about 2 feet above the plate, 2 feet high, and 17 inches across. The pitcher has to throw the ball inside this strike zone, but in a place where the batter can't hit it. If he throws it outside the strike zone, the batter may take a swing at it, but if he declines to, it's a ball. Four of them, and the batter goes to first base. This is the challenge a pitcher faces with each pitch. So how does he go about it?

As with almost everything in baseball, there is no simple answer. Of course pitchers and batters have strengths and weaknesses, and pitch selection will depend on these to a certain extent. If a pitcher's main strength is the knuckleball, for example, he's going to throw a lot of them. If it is widely known that a certain batter consistently has great difficulty with low curveballs over the outside part of the plate, you can be pretty sure that his diet will be heavy on curveballs low and away. But most major league hitters don't have such obvious weaknesses; most pitchers have several equally good pitches; and pitchers, catchers, and managers have to decide with each pitch what to throw. Deciding which pitch to use in a given situation is called *calling the game.* On most teams, it's the catcher who calls the game, informing the pitcher by use of hand signals what pitch he wants thrown. Some pitchers call their own games, signaling the catcher to let him know which pitch is coming. Some managers call an entire game; almost all of them call certain pitches at certain times. A pitchout—a ball placed deliberately far outside so that the catcher can stand up, grab it, and try to throw out a man stealing a base—is almost always called by the manager, who signals the catcher to call for the maneuver.

Kids start out pitching fastballs. The faster a ball goes, the harder it is to hit. By the time they're in high school or college, they can usually throw a curve, but they're less effective with it. So they'll stick with fastballs until the batter has two strikes on him, and then take a chance with a curve. A major league pitcher needs at least three effective pitches, so the change-up becomes important. Most major leaguers throw variations on these three pitches as well—slower or faster change-up, variations on the curve (sliders, screwballs), fastballs that have various kinds of movement—but we'll get into those details a bit later. For the moment, it is enough to say that a major league pitcher has a wide variety of effective pitches, and he has to choose one each time he winds up.

Calling the Game

So how do pitchers decide which pitch to throw? First, they have help: The catcher usually tells the pitcher what pitch he wants thrown, using signals with his fingers, hidden between his thighs so that the opposition can't see them, to indicate his choices. Every Little Leaguer knows that "one's a fastball; two's a curve," and it's true even in the major leagues that a catcher will call for a fastball by putting down one finger, a curve with two. Of course, the signs get a little more complicated when a pitcher has four or five different kinds of pitches and can place them in different parts of the strike zone, and more complicated still when a catcher has to change the signals because there are men on base who can see them. In any case, the catcher signals for a pitch, and the pitcher either agrees to pitch it or he "shakes him off"—refuses to use that particular pitch and asks for another signal. If you're not watching for a pitcher to shake off a sign, you'll probably never notice it's being done—the communication is as subtle as those auction bids at Sotheby's. Sometimes he'll do it with a tiny shake of his head, sometimes he'll just flick his glove slightly. Some pitchers nod when they've agreed to a pitch; some indicate their acceptance of the catcher's suggestion by simply throwing the pitch called for. Once the pitcher has agreed with the catcher, he winds up and throws. The catcher must know which pitch is coming. If the pitcher throws a fastball when the catcher is expecting a curve, the catcher may be unable to catch it.

Remember: The first pitch is important. If it's a strike, the chances of the batter getting a hit at all decline precipitously. Obviously, there are dozens of ways to choose a sequence—and equally obviously, you don't want to do it the same way every time so that the hitter will know what's coming. So imagine we're facing a right-handed hitter. We'll start him off with a fastball, a nice tight one on the inside part of the plate where it's hard to hit—but we're throwing it for a strike, so we can't use it to move him off the plate. He manages to get his bat on it and foul it off, but the job is done. We're ahead in the count, and we've got the hitter where we want him: We've got him thinking. He knows we've got a good fastball, so now what? A curveball low and away would be a fairly typical choice—hitters may suspect it's coming, but it works often enough anyway. This kind of curve looks like a fastball coming inside to a right-handed hitter, then it swings out over the plate for a low strike. But there are other possibilities, too. A change-up might work, because everyone saw that the batter had trouble with the fastball, and he's thinking another one's coming. A change will make him swing too soon—get "out in front" of the ball. Or we could just throw him another fastball inside—maybe he doesn't think that's coming simply because he expects some variety. Sometimes a fastball outside is a good idea—moving a fastball in and out is a good way to get some batters out. But that's what he's expecting, too. So let's throw another fastball inside. We throw, and the batter lunges to the outside, thinking that's where the pitch is going, and knowing that lunging into the ball is a good way to get power behind it. He misses it completely for strike two. Now he's swung at two fastballs. His timing is set for fastballs. Third pitch: the change-up. Fifteen miles an hour slower than the fastball, but it looks just like it when it comes out of the pitcher's hand. The batter is completely fooled, way out in front of the pitch—that is, swinging much too soon—and misses it for strike three. See how smart pitchers are, and how easy it is to get guys out? Yes—we're leaving out something here: The hitter, who is thinking all kinds of things himself and is nobody's fool. But let's save that for later. For now, let's examine what all the different pitches are and what they are supposed to do.

Fastballs

It's difficult to imagine how fast a major league fastball really is if you've never actually seen one coming at you. Home plate is 60 feet 6 inches away from the pitcher's rubber. The fastest major league pitchers can throw a ball with an initial velocity of ninety-seven miles per hour, sometimes slightly more. A ball with such a "muzzle velocity" will cross the plate, its speed reduced to ninety miles per hour, in .4 seconds. The batter must use this .4 seconds wisely. He must decide if the pitch is a fastball or a breaking ball, and plan to react accordingly. If it is an off-speed pitch, he must guess which way it will break. He must consider whether the ball is likely to pass within

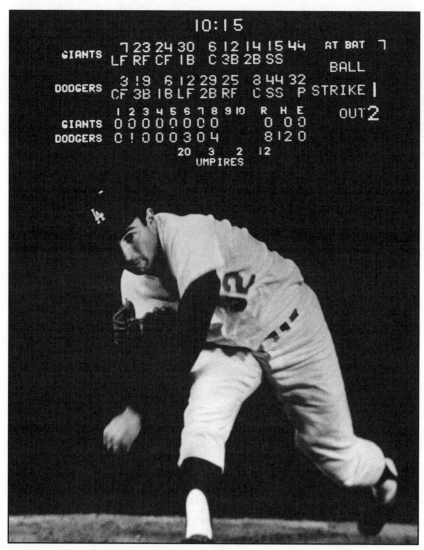

Sandy Koufax, one of the greatest fastball pitchers the game has ever known. The results of his efforts are apparent on the scoreboard—the Giants are about to become victims of another of Koufax's no-hit performances. *National Baseball Library & Archive, Cooperstown, NY*

the strike zone. If he decides it will, he must decide where in the strike zone it will pass and exactly how he might go about hitting it so that it falls where no one will catch it. If the batter is ahead in the count, he may have to decide to let a ball go by because, even though it is in the strike zone, he doesn't think he can hit it effectively. If he has two strikes on him, he may decide that he has to swing at this ball not because he can get a hit, but because he must foul it off to avoid striking out. Since all this thinking can't possibly go on in .4 seconds, the batter relies on guessing which pitch is coming and on quick reactions.

The best fastballs don't just go fast. They also have movement. If the pitcher places his index and middle fingers across the seams—the four-seam grip, as it's called—and if he can throw hard enough, the ball will "hop," or rise slightly. Put the index and middle fingers along the seams, where the seams come closest together, and the fastball will dip. The split-finger fastball, a pitch thrown with the index and middle fingers spread wide around the ball, sinks like a stone just as it enters the strike zone, often ending up in the dirt in front of the catcher. Some fastballs "tail off"—move slightly laterally at the end of their journey to the plate.

A good sinking fastball results in lots of ground balls and routine outs—batters tend to hit the top half of the ball, and the ball stays in the infield. A rising fastball causes hitters to swing under it and miss it completely, or catch the bottom half of the ball and pop it up.

If you ever do get to watch a ninety-mile-per-hour fastball up close, you will wonder (a) how anyone could throw something that fast using only his arm, and (b) how a batter even sees it, much less hits it. But they do hit it. In fact, many very good hitters prefer the fastball. They study pitchers carefully; they learn how a given pitcher's fastball moves; they try to guess when the fastball is coming; and they time their swings perfectly. If a pitcher threw nothing but fastballs at hitters like these, they would all be hitting .450 with 70 home runs. So pitchers throw other pitches too. This is called "changing speeds," and there are several ways to do it.

The Curveball and the Slider

These are the *breaking pitches*. By gripping the ball in a certain way, fingers placed just right in relationship to the seams on the baseball and using the wrist to put the proper spin on it, a ball can be thrown so that it actually curves—more than a foot when it's done right. What makes it even more confusing for the batter is that a good curve does most of its curving in the last 15 feet before it arrives at the plate. A curveball breaks down and away from a right-handed batter; a slider breaks in the same direction but closer to the plate and across rather than down. A variation of these pitches, called a *screwball*, breaks in the opposite direction. These pitches are thrown about ten or fifteen miles per hour slower than a fastball—but when the pitcher lets them go, they look exactly like a fastball. Any batter who is expecting a fastball when the curve comes will swing too early, swing where the ball isn't, or "lock up"—hesitate because his timing has been destroyed—and not swing at all as the ball passes through the strike zone. At least, that's the way the pitcher hopes things will turn out. It is one of the ancient truths of pitching that "the curveball makes the fastball effective" by creating this kind of confusion and doubt in the hitter.

> *"You know how you pitch to Mike Schmidt? Hard fastballs inside, sliders down and away. You know how you pitch Henry Aaron? Willie Mays? Hard stuff inside, soft away. You know how you pitch Willie Stargell? Hard stuff inside, soft away. You know how you pitch God? Hard stuff inside, then down and away, and if you get it there you'll get Him out. Even though He'll know it's coming. Or at least they say He knows."*
>
> —JIM LEFEBVRE, FORMER MAJOR LEAGUE INFIELDER AND MANAGER

The Change-up

This pitch looks just like the fastball when it's thrown, but the ball is palmed rather than held in the fingers, sometimes with the hand making the "OK" sign with the thumb and forefinger (the "circle change"). It comes straight toward the plate, but about ten to fifteen miles per hour slower than a fastball. Any hitter expecting a fastball and getting one of these will swing early and foul it off or miss it completely. The pitch is slow and easy to hit—provided the hitter is expecting it. But if he's guessing fastball, the change-up can make him look foolish. Most pitching coaches like to see the change-up thrown at the knees or below—hitters will often swing wildly at a change-up in the dirt. The pitcher must have a good fastball to complement the change-up, and the hitter must never know which one is coming.

The Knuckleball

Robert K. Adair, a Yale University physicist who wrote a fascinating book on the physics of baseball, had this to say about the knuckleball: "If the ball is thrown with very little rotation, asymmetric stitch configurations can be generated that lead to large imbalances of forces and extraordinary excursions in trajectory." In other words, the knuckleball is one weird pitch. The few pitchers who can throw it usually don't know where it's going to end up when it leaves their hands. Wild pitches are common: Catchers often wear specially designed extra-large mitts (but still within the guidelines set in The Book) to improve their chances of stopping it, which are not good. Bob Uecker, who caught Phil Niekro's knuckleball, used to say that the best way to catch it was to wait until it stopped rolling and then pick it up. So you can imagine what it does to the batter who has to find it and hit it.

> *"It actually giggles at you as it goes by."*
> —RICK MONDAY, DODGERS OUTFIELDER, ON PHIL NIEKRO'S KNUCKLEBALL

The pitch is usually thrown by digging the fingernails of the index and middle finger into the ball—knuckles have nothing to do with it. Unlike any other pitch, it comes at the batter with almost no

Charlie Hough is showing his age here in 1989—the strain on his face is that of a man in his forties playing a game meant for men in their twenties—but knuckleballers are long-lived. If you look closely, you can see his grip on the ball, with his fingernails digging into it. *National Baseball Library & Archive, Cooperstown, NY*

spin. Sometimes it breaks like a curveball, but it's just as likely to go up, down, in, or out. It seems incredible, but the pitch can actually change direction several times before it gets to the plate. Some believe that it doesn't work as well when the wind is behind the pitcher.

Throwing the knuckleball is easy on the arm. So those who throw it—if they do it well—can have long careers. Hoyt Wilhelm was 49 when he played his last major league game; Phil Niekro was 48; Ted Lyons was 45; Charlie Hough was 46.

The Spitball

Why are spitballs against the rules? Probably because they're so disgusting. Until 1920, the pitch was legal. Pittsburgh had an otherwise unmemorable pitcher called Marty O'Toole, who ended a five-year career with a 27–36 won-lost record, but who achieved a permanent place in the annals of grossness for his practice of sticking the ball right in his mouth and enthusiastically licking it before he threw. Then there was Burleigh Grimes, the last pitcher to use a legal spitball, who achieved the proper consistency and quantity of saliva by chewing the bark from an elm tree (which he found "tasty, really delicious") and then applying the resultant improved product to the ball in generous gobs. And this guy's in the Hall of Fame!

We do know that if a pitcher puts something slippery on the ball—Vaseline works well for those concerned about hygiene—the fingers slide off the ball more easily, and the ball will have less spin. Sometimes a spitball will look like a knuckleball; if it's thrown hard, it will resemble a split-finger fastball, sinking dramatically as it reaches the plate. It's impossible to say convincingly that a spitball gives an inferior pitcher an advantage—it's hard to throw a good spitball, just as it's hard to throw any other pitch well. Any major league pitcher needs a good fastball; but even when they were legal, not all pitchers threw spitballs or needed to, so it couldn't have been all that easy to do on the one hand, or offered that much of an advantage on the other. When in 1920 they allowed pitchers already using the pitch to continue to use it, only seventeen pitchers registered for the privilege.

Baseballs can be doctored in other, somewhat less revolting ways that will make them do strange things. Scuffing the ball with sandpaper or a nail file will cause it to curve toward the side of the ball that is scuffed. Of course, scuffing adds much smaller protrusions than the stitches, but enough to make the ball move a little more than it otherwise would, and enough to make it a little harder to hit. Scuffing the ball doesn't help everyone—you have to be a skilled pitcher to take advantage of the technique. And, of course, you have to be willing to cheat. Don Sutton had both qualifications. During a twenty-three-year career, mostly with the Los Angeles Dodgers, he won more than 300 games, and scuffed, cut, and otherwise retooled baseballs so thoroughly and with so many different implements that opposing players used to call him "Black and Decker."

Many more pitchers are accused, or suspected, of throwing illegal pitches than are actually ejected from games for doing so. Gaylord Perry, a 300-game winner who retired in 1983 after a twenty-two-year big league career, was one of the unhappy few who were actually thrown out of a game for putting gunk of some kind on the ball. It happened in 1982 when he was pitching for Seattle against Boston. Umpire Dave Phillips watched the bottom drop out of a pitch, and decided that Gaylord couldn't make a baseball do that without some sort of illegal help. He asked to see the ball, and found "some sort of slick substance" on it. He warned Perry that if it happened again, he'd throw him out of the game. Phillips was as good as his word. The next time he saw that sinker, Perry was on his way to the showers. When asked what kind of "slick substance" he found, Phillips said: "I'm an umpire, not a chemist." Perry appealed the decision to Lee McPhail, who, although he was not a chemist either, nevertheless fined Perry $250 and suspended him for ten days.

Baseball has often winked at spitballers, tolerated them, and laughed about their exploits. It even bestows its highest honor on some of the most notorious: Don Drysdale, Gaylord Perry, and Whitey Ford are all in the Hall of Fame.

Gaylord Perry is a Hall of Fame member who spent twenty-two years in the major leagues, and most people think he spent every last one of them throwing illegal spitballs. In 1982, he became one of the few pitchers actually ejected from a game for throwing a spitter. The umpire, Dave Phillips, said that he found "some slick substance" on the ball. When asked what kind, Phillips responded, "I'm an umpire, not a chemist." *National Baseball Library & Archive, Cooperstown, NY*

> *"You can't hit and think at the same time."*
> —YOGI BERRA

Sometimes just a reputation for throwing spitballs is enough to give the pitcher an advantage. Most pitchers feel that anything that adds to the batter's worries is useful, and that getting a batter to think about the possibility of a spitball, even a spitball that is never actually thrown, improves the chances of getting him out.

Throwing Inside

> *"I never hit anybody in the head intentionally. If a guy got hit on the head, it was his own fault. The head is the easiest part of the body to get out of the way. I hit guys in the ribs. The ribs don't move."*
> —BOB GIBSON

In addition to throwing various kinds of pitches, pitchers aim them toward certain parts of the strike zone in order to make them harder to hit. They move the ball in and out, depending on the hitter's strengths and weaknesses, and depending on the game situation. One essential part of locating pitches is throwing inside—near the batter. To hit the ball well, batters try to lean into the pitch and fully extend their arms, which puts more power behind the swing. Pitchers, naturally, try to discourage this practice. They do this by pitching inside, trying to "move the batter off the plate," make him lean back on his heels, and keep him from digging in his feet and extending his arms for a good swing. A ninety-mile-per-hour fastball that passes four inches from a batter's chin is not only very hard to hit, but may also persuade the batter to reconsider his plan to lean toward the plate on the next pitch. For good pitchers, pitching inside is part of a game plan, not an act of desperation or a piece of mindless cruelty. Pitchers correctly believe that they are under no moral obligation to turn over any more than a minimum share of the plate to a hitter. Batters may sometimes take offense, but when a .220 hitter charges the mound claiming that the pitcher is throwing at him—as seems to be happening frequently in recent years—well, somebody out there is flattering himself.

Still, pitching inside is controversial. There are subtle differences between various inside pitches. Pitching on the inside part of the plate is merely a tactic. A "purpose pitch" thrown very close to the batter, near his hands, is slightly more hostile, meant to convey a stronger message. And a beanball—thrown at the batter—is illegal, some even say criminal. Attempts to define the difference between these pitches can be the cause of much discussion, argument, and, occasionally, fisticuffs.

The Windup and the Set Position

You've seen a pitcher winding up—he raises both hands high above his head, pumps them back down, lifts his front leg high in the air, takes a big step forward, and finally throws the pitch, all in one smooth motion. You've also seen pitchers come to the set position, with the ball held with both hands in front of the chest, stop momentarily, check the runner on base (if there is one), and throw directly to the plate with one long stretch of the leg. When there are runners on base, threatening to steal, pitchers will use the set position instead of going through a big windup that will give runners extra time. With men on, a pitcher wants to deliver the ball to the plate as quickly as possible. Some pitchers use the set position all the time, even with no one on; most still like to wind up.

Changing Pitchers

The manager walks out of the dugout and strides toward the pitcher's mound. The catcher joins him there. He talks to the pitcher for a few seconds, and then waves his arm toward the bullpen. The pitcher puts the ball into the manager's hand and walks into the dugout. Why did the manager choose this moment to replace the pitcher? What did he see that you didn't?

According to the rules, pitchers get eight warm-up pitches from the mound when they start an inning or enter the game; according to custom, they'll tell the catcher what pitch they're throwing by using specific signs that are universal: 1. Palm toward the ground, airplane-taking-off motion: *fastball.* 2. Twist left wrist in counterclockwise (or right wrist in clockwise) direction: *breaking ball.* 3. Extend arm with ball in hand, wiggle it back and forth: *knuckleball.* 4. Extend arm with ball in hand, pull it toward chest: *change-up.* 5. Gesture over shoulder with gloved hand: *I'm done warming up, so throw the ball to the second baseman after this pitch.*

There are, of course, certain special situations that would make a manager yank a pitcher who was doing well—he's a lefty, it's late in a close game, and there's a righty coming up to bat, for example. Or there's a batter coming up who has a record of hitting this particular pitcher very well. But sometimes things like this don't apply—it's just that the manager has seen something that causes him to doubt the pitcher's ability to continue. Of course, often that "something" is obvious—there are lots of batters getting hits, and the pitcher isn't getting anybody out. But managers want to pull a pitcher out before such disasters occur. According to Earl Weaver, the great former manager of the Baltimore Orioles, there are a number of things an observant manager will be looking for—and the observant fan can see them, too.

First, watch foul balls. If the batters are fouling the ball straight back, it's nothing to worry about. But if they're hitting fouls down the lines, that means they're getting around on the pitches, and the pitcher is probably losing velocity. Keep your eye on the catcher: If you see him glance toward the dugout, that means he's worried. He has sensed something in the pitcher's delivery that isn't right. Third, see how long the pitcher pauses between pitches. Some pitchers take longer than others, but if you see him slowing down, he's getting tired. Fourth, a leadoff walk is trouble. Walks in other situations might be excusable, but walking the leadoff hitter may mean the pitcher is losing his control. Next, watch the batters at the bottom of the lineup. If these weak hitters are pulling the ball, the pitcher is going to be taking a shower soon. If the pitcher is a sinker-ball pitcher throwing high out of the strike zone, he's in trouble. If he's wild with low pitches, it's probably something he can get under control before it's too late. And seventh and last, see if you can detect any awkwardness in the pitcher's motion, anything different from what he was doing at the start of the game. A pitcher who is pitching well will usually look exactly the same with every pitching motion—if you start seeing variations, he's tired.

Watch carefully and always try to beat the manager to the punch. When the manager fails to obey your instructions to replace the pitcher (delivered loudly enough for all your companions to hear) and then the next batter gets a hit, just shrug your shoulders, rest your chin on your hand, and gaze toward heaven. No need to rub it in.

CATCHING

The catcher is the only player on the field who carries more than a glove. He wears hard plastic shin guards, a padded chest protector, and a steel-barred mask, padded with leather near his face and strapped over the back of his head. He also wears a hard batting helmet, with the brim turned around backward—not to make a fashion statement, but to make room for the mask and to protect his skull from fast-moving hard objects. The catcher is routinely clonked with foul tips, pitches in the dirt, and occasionally even the bat of the opposing hitter. When you see him crouch behind the plate waiting for the pitch, you'll notice that he usually hides his bare hand behind his leg—bruised knuckles and smashed fingernails are the catcher's lot, and he tries to minimize them by putting one of the few unprotected parts of his body out of harm's way. It's interesting that whenever a baseball player is injured, even very slightly, the trainer and manager will rush out onto the field, all furrowed brows and worried looks. But when a catcher is smashed in the elbow by a foul tip off a ninety-six-mile-an-hour fastball, he writhes on the ground in agony all by himself. Catchers are supposed to get creamed, and no one seems concerned, or even especially surprised, when they do. Catching is so physically demanding that most teams carry three catchers, substituting them for each other when they're injured, or even when they're just tired out. The most durable catchers—Johnny Bench, Bob Boone, or Carlton Fisk, for example— rarely played more than about 135 games out of the 162-game schedule; and only three catchers—Bob Boone, Gary Carter, and Carlton Fisk—have caught more than 2,000 games. It's just too hard on the body. Fisk, who caught 2,226 games in a twenty-three-year career, broke his legs and several ribs, had ligaments torn away from his pelvic bone, and had the cartilage in his knee surgically repaired.

The catcher is peculiar in other ways as well. He's the only player on the field with a perfect view of all the other players, so he's often in charge of telling other players where to position themselves. He's the only player who, in normal play, assumes a position in foul territory. He's usually the most muscular man on the team—he squats down to receive pitches around 140 times every game, which certainly helps to build up the thigh muscles.

Qualifications for the Job

In addition to being extremely durable and almost completely insensitive to pain, a catcher has to have a good arm—second base, the most common place for a catcher to make a play, is 127 feet away. This is not a vast distance for a major league player—

outfielders regularly throw the ball 250 feet and more on a fly—but to get a runner out, the throw has to be unloaded fast and thrown extremely accurately. It has to be placed in exactly the right position to catch a sliding runner—if it's even a little off, or a fraction of a second late, the runner will be safe.

Although most catchers are notoriously slow runners, it certainly doesn't hurt to have some speed afoot. Catchers back up plays to first (under certain circumstances), which means they're running down the first base line many times a game. Many of them may seem chunky and awkward, but actually they have to be agile enough to spring from a crouch, grab a bunt, and throw a man out at first in one smooth motion. And they have to do it with all the equipment weighing them down.

Speed and gracefulness are required in other parts of the job, too. One of the most obvious jobs of the catcher (when there are men on base) is to make sure that no pitches get past him. If they do, the men on base can advance, even score, on a wild pitch (if the pitcher threw wildly) or passed ball (if the catcher missed a pitch he should have caught). Remember how fast baseballs are coming at him: .4 seconds from the pitcher's hand to the catcher's glove. This is not a lazy game of catch: He has to know in advance where every pitch is going, how to position himself to receive it, and how it will bounce in the event it hits the dirt in front of him. If you watch closely, you'll see the catcher positioning himself for each pitch— and you can sometimes guess where the pitch is going by how he shuffles his feet. This foot shuffling and repositioning has to be done carefully, and as late as possible before the pitch is thrown: The catcher doesn't want the other team to know where the pitch is go- ing. A curveball in the dirt will bounce differently from a fastball in the dirt. The catcher has to know what's coming; he has to know what will happen when a given pitch goes astray; and he has to be ready for everything.

Catching a high pop-up near or behind the plate is another of his jobs. Watch him go after a pop-up. His first move is to his mask— he pulls it off so that he can see what he's doing. (Gary Carter, who caught for the Mets and the Expos, would, like many catchers, occasionally play another position so that he could rest while still keeping his bat in the lineup. He once went after a pop-up while he was playing first base. His first move was to reach up, and, as if he had a mask on, push his hat right off his head. Obviously, it becomes a reflex.) Once the catcher has his mask off, he doesn't drop it on the ground. Instead, he holds on to it until he's sure he knows where he's going to make the catch, then he heaves it 15 feet away. The last thing he wants to do is stumble over his mask just as he's pulling in the ball. After getting rid of the mask, he seems to stagger around under the ball, sometimes chasing it right back to the edge of the field-level seats, where he will try to deprive some fan of a souvenir. Some catchers have perfected a spectacular technique for catching pop-ups near the wall without hurting themselves: They slide like a runner sliding into a base just as they get to the wall, simultaneously catching the ball and hitting the wall with their feet. Sometimes you'll see the catcher shuffling over near the dugout, right to the top of the steps, his head raised, eyes determinedly on the ball, apparently unaware that he's about to take a header down four steps into a puddle of tobacco juice on the concrete floor. If it's his own dugout, his teammates will be there to catch him, of course, but only after he makes the catch and not a second before. If it's the visiting team's dugout that he's inching toward, he can't expect much help. Instead, you'll see him take a quick look to find the steps and make a rough estimate of how painful the fall will be.

In addition to physical skills, catching requires personality. A catcher has to get along well with umpires, a skill whose value should not be underestimated. He has the most intimate relationship of any player with the man in blue, and he is, at least tacitly, pleading his case on every pitch. He does this, partly, by "framing" pitches—catching the ball in such a way that a pitch that might well be called a ball looks like a strike to the umpire because of the way he moves his catcher's mitt to gather it in. He also has to be a charmer with pitchers, knowing when to flatter, when to scold, when to just shut up and catch. He has to know his pitchers well enough to perceive the slightest indication that something may be wrong with the way they're throwing, and he must understand what to do to correct the problem.

Throwing Runners Out

Base stealing—and we'll discuss this at length elsewhere—is one of the most exciting plays in baseball. The catcher's role in it is, of course, central. Most attempts to steal second result in success—the runner makes it safely. But, statistically, a base stealer has to be successful at least 67 percent of the time in order to do his team more good than harm. So any catcher who can throw out more than about a third of the runners who try to steal on him is doing his job. But this is not easy. If a catcher can catch the ball, jump up, release it, and make the 127-foot throw to second base all in the space of 2 seconds, he's only average. He's good if he can do it in 1.9 seconds. At least one catcher, Benito Santiago of the Padres, can do it in 1.8— probably because he has such a rifle for an arm that he can throw from his knees and still get runners out.

Of course, second base isn't the only place catchers throw to. A pickoff to first, while not often attempted, is a beautiful play to watch. A catcher has to watch what base runners are doing, and if he sees a runner with a larger lead than normal, or if something else about the runner's demeanor suggests that he is about to steal, he'll react. In making a play to first, usually the catcher will call for a pitchout on a right-handed batter—that is, he'll tell the pitcher (by means of the signs mentioned earlier) to throw the ball far outside. He'll step up as the pitch is thrown and whip the ball to first, all in one smooth motion. Occasionally, a catcher will throw to first after receiving a normal pitch—this because he feels he's caught the runner on first not paying attention, or ambling back toward the bag instead of moving fast. That's a play that's very hard to see coming, but once in a while an astute fan who is really paying attention can see a runner at first about to be caught with his pants down. Obviously, this play requires considerable alertness on the part of the first baseman as well.

Out at Home

This is the big play for the catcher. Like the goalie on your daughter's field hockey team, he's the last obstacle to scoring, and therefore the center of attention for the biggest defensive play in the game: tagging someone out at the plate. This play at home is one of the few contact plays in baseball, and blocking the plate, sometimes at the sacrifice of physical well-being, is one of the catcher's jobs. It is the runner's job on this play to crash into the catcher, hoping to jar the ball loose and score a run.

Why is it that runners crash into the catcher, but almost never into anyone covering second or third? There are plenty of times, on non-force plays, where crashing into a second baseman or third baseman might have the same effect as crashing into a catcher—knocking the ball loose, with good results for the runner. But it isn't done. Why? You might want to try this one on some baseball expert you know. He'll probably flop around trying to find an explanation in the rules, but there's nothing in The Book to help him. The explanation is more subtle than the black and white of the rule book. Baseball has a six-month season, with a game almost every day. Smashing up your body, whether by running into walls in the outfield or running into fielders at the bases, is risky business. In football, by contrast, smashing yourself up to make a big play may be good tactics: There are only sixteen games in a season anyway, and a single big play can make a season. Besides, you've got a week to recover from an injury. In baseball, you have to play tomorrow night, and the night after that too. The reason players are willing to risk injury by smashing into a catcher is because home plate is worth more than other bases. It just isn't worth it for any other base, so players sensibly don't risk it.

FIRST BASE

A batter hits a sharp grounder to the left of the third baseman, who makes a spectacular diving stop. He hops to his feet, spins around, makes the long throw across the diamond, and nips the runner at first. The guy at first who catches the ball doesn't get much attention on a play like this—he's just standing where the agile third baseman throws the ball.

First base is sometimes thought of as a place to put a clumsy fielder who can help your team with his bat, but this may be less true now than it once was. Even if a play like the one just described is pretty simple, it's no reason to take the first baseman for granted. This is a position that, like all the others, requires considerable thought, solid baseball instincts, and tremendous physical skill.

The first baseman is usually left-handed. With the glove on the right hand, he's in a better position to slap a tag on a runner on the pickoff play, and in a much better position to throw to second or third when picking up a bunt or a grounder. Look at the first baseman the next time you're at a game—lefty Don Mattingly is one of the best first basemen of recent years—and watch how he has to move: It's easy to see that a first baseman who throws with his left hand and catches with his right fits properly with the shape of the field and the location of the other players. There have of course been many right-handed first basemen, including some very good ones—Vic Power, Gil Hodges, and Rod Carew come to mind. But take a look around—usually you'll see a lefty at first.

With no runners on base, the first baseman will position himself behind and to the left of the base (from the batter's point of view). From here, he's ready both to field balls hit to the right side of the infield and to cover first base for the putout on a throw from one of the other infielders. (When the first baseman fields a grounder, the pitcher must cover first. In fact, dashing over to first base when a ball is hit to the right side of the infield has to be a reflex in pitchers.) With no one on, a first baseman will play far enough from the base so that he has to run to get to the base to receive the throw—playing that far away ensures that he'll have the necessary range to properly field the position. So with no one on, things are simple enough.

"Catching the ball is a pleasure. Knowing what to do with it is a business."

—TOMMY HENRICH

But with men on, it gets complicated. It's fun to watch the first baseman and try to think along with him. Let's say there's a man on first, nobody out. Everyone in the infield is thinking double play, and how they're going to do their part if called upon. The first baseman has the additional job of holding the runner on base—if he steals second, there'll be no double play possibility to think about. So he moves from his position to the left and behind the bag, and holds the runner on.

Holding the Runner on Base

With his right foot next to the bag and his left foot along the baseline, the first baseman opens his glove and faces the pitcher, waiting for the pickoff throw. When it comes, he swipes it across the bag, trying to catch the runner diving or sliding back. Then he returns the ball to the pitcher and resumes his position. If the runner is really a threat to steal, a pitcher might throw over four, five, six times or more before he pitches. This makes some fans nuts—they want the pitcher to throw the damn ball at the batter and get it over with. But don't be too hasty. This cat-and-mouse game with the runner at first is more than just an attempt to pick him off, which rarely succeeds anyway. It's more important as a way to make the runner hold back— just a little—so that he can be nailed at second when the time comes, or to make him reluctant to steal at all. The tolerances here are very small; a fraction of a second, a half-step is enough to allow the infielders to turn a double play that otherwise wouldn't happen. So although this may look like a futile game of catch between pitcher and first baseman, it isn't. Throwing over enough to make the runner stick a fraction closer to the bag can be enough to make a big difference: the difference between no one on with two outs, and man on first with one out.

Of course, the first baseman is doing more here than holding the runner on. He still has to be a fielder, so when the pitch is made, he bounds off the base to get ready to field a ball hit to the right side. He's also thinking about balls hit to the outfield—he's going to be the cutoff man if a ball is hit to right field, and he has to remember that role as well. So in case there's a double hit down the right field line, he has to be thinking about how he's going to make the judgment about stopping a throw to the plate or letting it go through. He knows he'll have to keep his eye on the runner when he's rounding third and at the same time listen to his teammates' instructions about what to do with the throw when it comes his way.

The double play is a bit more complicated for the first baseman than for other infielders. Any other fielder who picks up a grounder when there's a runner on first knows that his play is to second base. But the first baseman has a decision to make if the ball is hit his way. He can throw to second, of course, and get the lead runner. But then he has to hustle back to first to finish the double play—or let his pitcher take the throw to first. The 3–6–3 double play (first baseman to shortstop to first baseman) is difficult to execute properly, and the 3–6–1, where the pitcher covers first, is probably even harder.

Suppose, though, that the first baseman picks up the grounder right near the base. He can then step on first and throw to second. But he has to remember that now the runner going to second isn't forced—the shortstop covering second has to tag him to get him out. Because touching second base is no longer enough, he's made the shortstop's job in completing the double play that much more difficult.

Sometimes you'll see a first baseman playing slightly away from the bag with a man on, inching up just enough to keep the runner honest, and then moving away again. Especially with a lefty at bat (or with a righty to whom the pitcher is throwing outside fastballs), when a ball hit to the right side can therefore be expected, the first baseman wants to make sure that nothing gets past him. At the same time, he doesn't want the runner to get a decent lead. So he compromises.

Intimate Relationships

A first baseman interacts especially with two particular teammates: the second baseman and the pitcher. With no one on, the first baseman is another fielder on the right side. If a ball is hit that way, the second baseman and the first baseman have to decide who will pick it up. On most teams, the second baseman is in charge of this play: If he says he's got it, the first baseman backs off. But who is covering first while this little interaction is going on between the first and second baseman? The pitcher. On every ball hit to the right side of the infield, the pitcher heads for first to cover the base. Usually he won't have to take the throw—either the first baseman is covering the bag for the throw from the second baseman, or he has picked up the ball and gone to the base himself to make the play unassisted. But on other occasions, the pitcher will take the throw from the first baseman, simultaneously finding first base with his foot and making the putout. Usually the first baseman shovels the ball to him underhanded, leading him toward the base with his toss. A first baseman's work is never done: If there are men on base when all this is happening, then he has to watch them, too, and tell the pitcher where to throw (or not throw) the ball after the pitcher makes the putout.

The Big Stretch

The typical picture of a first baseman has him stretching with leg and arm toward a throw from an infielder, his back foot touching the side of the base. Of course, the sooner a ball gets to the first baseman, the better the chance of a putout; and stretching out like that is one way to make the ball arrive sooner. This is such a common idea—you see Little League first basemen imitating this gesture all the time—that some fans may forget that it isn't done all that often. In fact, stretching out like that puts you in a vulnerable position—if the throw is slightly off, you don't have time to adjust and make the catch. So first basemen use that maneuver only when absolutely necessary—that is, when the play is very close, and when they're sure that the throw is perfectly on line. Nobody wants to be caught in a graceful stretch while the ball sails over his glove and into the dugout, however impressive that posture may look on the front of a baseball card.

SECOND BASE AND SHORTSTOP

These two are called the middle infielders, and they form the keystone of a team's defense. Pitchers love these guys, and the reason is simple: the double play. This elegant pas de deux, which these two are almost always responsible for, is one of the most graceful plays in all of sports, and truly the pitcher's best friend. With one batted ball, you can go from nobody out and one on to two out and nobody on. The double play not only gets the batter but also erases the pitcher's previous mistake—allowing the runner to get to first. It's the rally-killer that every pitcher hopes for.

First, watch the middle infielders' positions in a double play situation. You'll see them "cheat in" a step or two in order to be able get to the base a little faster and pick up a grounder a little earlier. There's a risk, of course—it's easier to field a fast ground ball from farther back, but the risk is worth it if it gets you two outs at once.

> *"Next to the triple play, baseball's double play is the most exciting and graceful thing in sports."*
> —ALISTAIR COOKE

The double play can be started by either of them. (Of course, it can be started by any other player as well, but most of them begin with one of these two.) When the second baseman starts it, there are a half dozen different ways he can do it. If the ball is hit near enough to the bag, the second baseman steps on the base and throws to first. If it's hit to his right, but too far from the bag for him to step on it, he'll toss it underhand to the shortstop covering second. A ball hit directly at him can be handled with a neat backhand toss to the shortstop, who is covering second base. On this play, and on balls hit to his left, he might also use a pivot—twist his shoulders toward second base, often dropping to one knee to make sure he's in the right position, and then throw. On a slow roller, he can run in, pick it up, tag the runner going by, and then throw to first. Runners, of course, will try not to cooperate with this last technique, usually by stopping short and making the second baseman come after them.

When the shortstop fields the ball, on the left side of the infield, his choices are more limited. If he's close enough, he can step on second himself and throw to first. Or he can toss to the second baseman covering second. But if the ball is hit to his left, he usually won't be able to make a double play: He's moving in the wrong direction, and it is unlikely that he will be able to stop, turn, and throw fast enough. It isn't impossible, though, and he will certainly want to try at least to get the lead runner with a throw to second. On slow grounders, or balls hit considerably to his left, he may have to settle for the third and worst choice: the throw to first that gets that runner, but leaves a man on second. One of the best shortstops ever is still playing today: It may be worth a detour to St. Louis to watch Ozzie Smith demonstrate how the position of shortstop should be played.

PIVOT MEN

This is the name (usually applied to second basemen) for the man who takes the ball at second, steps on the bag, and throws on to first. It is one of the great plays in all of baseball, and a great pivot man—

Bill Mazeroski, Willie Randolph, and Joe Morgan are good examples from the past—is a joy to watch. Mazeroski, who is perhaps better known by some fans for his World Series–ending home run against the Yankees in 1960, is remembered by connoisseurs of the double play for his ability to catch the ball and throw it on to first so quickly and smoothly that it seemed as if he hardly even touched it. (Umpires give pivot men the benefit of doubt; on instant replays, it is often clear that the pivot man was not actually holding the ball and touching second base at the same time.) Today, watch Jody Reed of the Padres, Baltimore's Roberto Alomar, and Carlos Baerga

Willie Randolph, a master of the pivot at second base. He would float gracefully across the base, hardly seeming to touch the ground at all; then the ball would fly toward first base almost before you knew he had it—a kind of sleight of hand that only the best pivot men can master. *Bettmann Archive*

in Cleveland if you want to see how it should be done. A pivot man needs not only grace, but courage. The runner is sliding into him as hard as possible, hoping to knock him over and ruin his throw. The pivot man has to ignore the runner until his throw is safely away. Then he can jump out of the way or over the sliding runner, the final flourish at the end of his act. Sometimes it seems as if the pivot man made his throw while he was actually in the air leaping over the sliding runner, but this is almost never the case. Every fan should watch the pivot man on the double play, and watch him closely. This is one of the great moments of artistry during a baseball game, and it merits close attention.

THE HIT-AND-RUN AND THE STOLEN BASE

So far, so good: balls hit to the right side, shortstop covers second for the DP; balls hit to the left, second baseman covers. But we're forgetting something: There's a guy on first base who might steal, or go on a hit-and-run—that is, start running as soon as the pitch is made, even before the batter makes contact with the ball—precisely to eliminate the double play possibility. So who's supposed to cover second if that happens? Now the second baseman and the shortstop have to make some decisions.

The worst thing that can happen in this situation is that the middle infielder vacates his position to cover the bag, and the batter hits the ball right at the spot just vacated. When this happens, instead of the double play you wanted, or the one out you would have settled for, everyone's safe, and it's men on first and third. How can this be avoided? Knowing in advance where the hitter will hit the ball would help. Although no predictions will be perfect, there are ways to guess with a high degree of accuracy where the ball will be hit and to plan accordingly.

Guessing correctly involves several factors. First, is the hitter a lefty or a righty? Righties tend to hit toward the left side; lefties toward the right. Not all of them, but most of them. Second, where is the next pitch going to be thrown? If the pitcher plans an outside fastball to a right-handed hitter, it's likely to be hit toward the right. If he's throwing an inside curve, it's more likely to be hit to the left side. No guarantees—just probability. Third, what are the tendencies of this particular hitter? If he's a consistent pull hitter (that is, a lefty who hits to right or a righty who hits to left), then you'll have a pretty good idea that he'll do it again. You can't be sure, of course, but it's one more factor to add to the equation. So the second baseman and the shortstop have information to work with: They can see whether the batter is hitting lefty or righty; they know what pitch is coming because they can see the catcher's sign; and they are aware from prior experience of this particular hitter's tendencies. They weigh the possibilities and make a decision, using reasoning that might go something like this: This batter is a lefty who consistently pulls the ball; but the pitcher is throwing an outside fastball, and this guy has trouble getting his bat around on fastballs. The last time up, he grounded a fastball to the left side, contrary to his habit of pulling the ball, because he swung late. He's never been able to hit this pitcher's fastball solidly; he'll probably swing late this time, too. Conclusion: He's going to hit it to the left side of the infield. That means the shortstop will have to stay where he is to field the ball, and the second baseman will cover the base.

Of course, this decision has to be arrived at between the shortstop and second baseman with each batter and before each pitch. And they have to communicate with each other—it would be pretty embarrassing, to say the least, to find themselves both covering the base, or neither covering, when the throw comes from the catcher. So they have a simple way of talking to each other, which you can see if you look closely. Usually the shortstop makes the decision and communicates it to the second baseman. You'll see him hold his glove up to his face and turn toward his left. Behind the glove, safe from the prying eyes of the opposition, he is either holding his mouth wide open or tightly closed. Closed means "I'll cover." Open means "You cover." Keeping this communication secret is important, because a good hitter can direct his hit left or right. You want to keep him guessing about which side of the infield is going to be open. Simple enough—but it took quite a bit of information, processed very quickly, to arrive at the correct decision. This is a time when the alert fan is thinking and watching intently. The sign only takes a split second just before the pitch—watch for it the next time you see a man on first in a situation where a steal is likely.

THIRD BASE

Baseball clichés are an essential part of the game, and you have to know the cliché nickname for third base: the *hot corner*. Third base requires an athlete with fast feet and a powerful arm. The play on which he moves to his right, snags a ball as he falls past the third base foul line, and then turns and throws to first is one of the most difficult defensive plays in the game. Watching the best third basemen make this play is astonishing and delightful. If you ever get a chance to see films of Brooks Robinson or Mike Schmidt doing this, you will know what I mean. Among third basemen to watch closely today are Ken Caminiti of the Padres, Matt Williams of the Giants, and the Chicago White Sox's Robin Ventura.

The routine play for a third baseman is a grounder picked up neatly and a fast, long throw to first. He doesn't need the range of a shortstop or a second baseman—the ground he needs to cover is more limited. He sometimes starts a double play. And he does have another fancy play to make besides the one previously described: He has to defend against the bunt by running in, grabbing it with his bare right hand—third basemen are always righties, the mirror image of the usually left-handed first baseman—and making an underhand throw all the way across to first. Arguably, there are more tough chances at third than at any other infield position.

There's a good reason why it's called the hot corner. Of the four infielders, the third baseman plays closest to the plate, so the ball gets to him faster than it does to anyone else. He has to be quick on his feet to both left and right. He often has to dive into the dirt to catch a ball, and he has to come up throwing hard—he's the infielder farthest from first base. Most third basemen feel that their reactions have to be so fast that they're reflexive, and it certainly looks that way to a spectator. Many third basemen claim that they've never been afraid of getting a hardball in the teeth—Robinson, Boggs, and others have said as much—but it does occasionally happen, and the danger of a fast line drive or a grounder that takes a bad hop must at least occur to them. It certainly occurs to the spectator watching a major league third baseman at work. In 1948, George Kell, playing third for the Detroit Tigers, caught a Joe DiMaggio line smash with his face, breaking his jaw. Kell picked up the ball, touched third for the force-out, and then passed out cold. Try watching the third baseman as the pitch is thrown; see him bounce up on the balls of his feet, pound his glove, and lean over, staring at the batter. Then imagine what must be going through his mind. Now imagine what goes through his mind when he charges the plate, getting ready to play the bunt, knowing that the batter might just decide instead to swing away, right into his face.

The third baseman has to reposition himself more often than any other infielder, depending on who is batting. Against a pull hitter, you'll see him playing right on the foul line, trying to prevent a double down the line. When his team is ahead by a few runs, he'll move over to his left a bit more, on the theory that with a decent lead, it's more important to prevent the more common single between short and third than the possible double down the line. He'll also be thinking about a half dozen or so other factors in deciding where to plant his feet: Is the batter likely to bunt? Is my pitcher a good fielder? Is the batter a fast or slow runner? How fast is the infield (that is, is there high grass or wet turf that will slow the ball down, or an AstroTurf surface that will speed it up)? And what am I supposed to do if there's a hit to the outfield? Am I the cutoff man? Where am I supposed to throw the ball once I catch it? Watch the third baseman pacing around and readjusting before each pitch, especially when there are men on base or it's a bunt situation.

Each situation presents another problem for the third baseman. If he has a runner on first and less than two outs, he'll be thinking about the bunt—and what to do with the ball once he picks it up. If the runner is slow enough, he'll want to go to second with the throw— it's almost always best to get the lead runner. On the other hand, if his team has a good lead, or the runner is very fast, he'll want to get the sure out and throw to first. Sometimes he'll know the bunt is coming—say, with fewer than two out and runners on first and second in a game where the score is close or tied—so he'll move in toward the plate. Yet he'll still have to see if the pitcher can field the bunt, in which case he'll head for third base to cover for the force play. If a grounder comes his way near third, he'll step on the base and relay to first for the double play. With bases loaded, he'll throw home for the force, and the catcher will go to first for the double play. If the ball is hit to his left, he'll go to second to start the double play. We're still not done: Suppose that there's a man on second with less than two out. He'll field the grounder, hold it for a moment to make sure that the man on second can't advance, and then throw to first just in time to get the runner. Man on third, less than two outs? Hold the runner tight—you don't want him stealing home, and if you field the ball, you want to hold it long enough to prevent him from breaking for the plate; then the long throw to first. With two out and a man on third, he might still try to steal, though it's less likely. So you can ignore him if you pick up a grounder, and just go to first with your throw. As you can see, there are a considerable number of possibilities, and the third baseman has to be making these evaluations and decisions before every pitch.

LEFT FIELD

"He's way out in left field," we say of someone who seems confused, distracted, or otherwise out of it. And in fact left field is on some teams a kind of halfway house for a player whose bat you need, but whose fielding skills leave something to be desired. Traditionally, it is a refuge for the weak arm or the clumsy glove. This may be why you never hear anyone say, "He's way out in center field," even though center field is in some sense more way out than left.

But for every weak-armed Luis Polonia, there's a Rickey Henderson or Barry Bonds who plays left field with skill and grace. So be careful what you say when you accuse someone of being out in left field. And if you're talking to a Red Sox fan, don't ever say that the left fielder is an oaf. Playing left in Fenway Park, with the big green wall at your back, is one of the trickier positions in the majors, and the list of Red Sox who've played there over the past fifty years— Ted Williams, Carl Yastrzemski, Jim Rice, Mike Greenwell—makes a pretty good start for a Boston Red Sox Hall of Fame.

Nevertheless, it is true that the left fielder doesn't need as good an arm as the other outfielders. His longest throw is to home, and most of his throws are to second or third base. It's the center fielder who has to have speed and range—he's always assigned more ground to cover. And the right fielder needs a better arm to throw accurately to third base. The most important job for the left fielder is to field cleanly so that runners can't take a base on him, stretching a single into a double. Fast runners who've hit a single to left field will watch the left fielder closely—even a momentary bobble or hesitation on his part will send them tearing for second base; remember, it's much easier to score from second than from first, so it's worth it to the runner to challenge the left fielder when he can. When a left fielder is known for having a weak arm, runners will be that much more eager to run on him. The left fielder can compensate with some speed. You'll notice that a weak-armed left fielder will play in close to make his throw shorter for balls hit in front of him, and then count on his speed afoot to go back on fly balls hit over his head. He'll also use his speed to catch up with hits down the line, turning doubles into singles, and triples into doubles.

RIGHT FIELD

The right fielder needs the strongest arm of all the outfielders. His throw to third can be even more important than the throw home—it's the throw that prevents a runner from even trying to go to third from second. (It is, as we've seen, extremely difficult to prevent a run from scoring when there's a man on third with fewer than two out.) He usually doesn't have to make a throw to second—most runners feel it's too risky to try to stretch a single to right field into a double. If one does try to run, however, the right fielder needs to be able to throw strongly and accurately to get him out. Runners are afraid of the best right field arms—just knowing there's a good arm out there will keep them on first. Dwight Evans, who played a long career in right field for the Red Sox, used to make a point of warming up before every game by taking infield ground balls and making long hard throws to first. He wanted to make sure the opposition saw that he had an arm and knew how to use it. If you want to see the way right field should be played, try to catch some films of Roberto Clemente, the Pirates' right fielder in the 1960s. He was famous for wall-crashing catches, but his throwing arm was even more extraordinary.

CENTER FIELD

Center is usually reserved for one of the best athletes on the team. He needs both physical skills and knowledge of the game. He has the largest territory to cover, and he's in charge of who gets to catch what. The center fielder's job is to take any ball that he can get to—when he calls for something, the other two outfielders make way for him. On balls hit "in the gap"—between outfielders—he has to communicate with the other fielder concerning who is going to take it. If there's any question about who the ball is closer to, the center fielder must take it, and the left or right fielder must back him up. If the outfielders are doing their jobs properly, you'll see them all in motion on every ball hit to the outfield—if an outfielder isn't actually catching the ball, then he's running to back up the one who is. The center fielder has an additional backup job: He has to cover the throw from the catcher to second on an attempted steal. If the throw from the catcher is wild, the runner will be safe at second, and that's the catcher's fault. But if the runner makes it to third, blame the center fielder. He should have been there to cover and prevent it.

Playing Deep, Playing Shallow

Some outfielders—Dave Winfield was known for this—like to play shallow. This makes it easier on the arm when it's time for a throw, and going back fast on a ball to the fence—let's face it—draws some cheers, a form of flattery no professional baseball player (nor any of the rest of us, for that matter) is immune to. But there's more than personal preference or desire for approval involved in outfield positioning. It's a matter of strategy.

Even as high as the lower levels of the minor leagues, most outfielders just play straight away—that is, the left fielder lines up between second and third, the right fielder between first and second, and the center fielder a little to the left or right of the pitcher, so that he can see the hitter. But by the time you get to the majors, you have pitchers who can put the ball in a specific part of the strike zone, and hitters and runners whose tendencies are well known. These factors will affect positioning. When a batter is behind in the count—as you recall—he becomes a much worse hitter. Outfielders will move in a step or two, and move a step left on a lefty, a step right on a righty. In protecting the plate on an 0–2 pitch, hitters are more likely to hit to the opposite field. When the count is 2–0 and sometimes when it's 3–0, you'll see outfielders backing up: This is when a hitter is going to take a good healthy swing at the ball.

The game situation is also important. With the potential tying or go-ahead run on second late in the game, the aim is to prevent the runner from scoring on a single; so outfielders will play shallow enough that they'll be able to throw a runner out at the plate. This risks allowing a double over your head, but so what? A double (or even a long single) will score the runner anyway, no matter where you're playing. On the other hand, with the potential tying or go-ahead run on first, a single usually won't score the runner, but a double will. So play deep, give up the single that you might have caught on a fly if you were playing shallow, and prevent the run-scoring double. It all makes sense when you weigh the consequences. Try thinking about outfield positioning next time you're at a game—it's always great to tell the guy next to you that the left fielder should be playing closer in, and then, on the next pitch, see a run score on a single because he was playing too deep to make the throw to the plate. Try not to smirk, and never say "I told you so"—that would be bush league.

3

Offense—and How to Stop It

When scouts go out looking for major league talent, they are usually looking for five qualities. They want a man who can run, field, throw, hit for power, and hit for average. With four of these, you can still make it in the majors, particularly if one really stands out. With only three, you have to be pretty terrific at all of them. And if you only have two, well, you'd better find some other line of work. Dave Kingman, an outfielder and first baseman for the Mets, the A's, and other teams in the 1970s and 1980s, had a miserable .236 lifetime average, but he hit 442 home runs. His power was enough to make up for regularly striking out about 130 times a season. One year with the Mets, he only hit .204, but topped the league with 37 home runs. And he was consistent right to the end. In his last season, when he was mainly a designated hitter with Oakland, he provided a rare example of a full-time player with real skills in only one of the five categories: He played the field rarely and then without distinction, tried stealing six bases and got caught three times, hit .210 and clonked 35 homers. His poor averages certainly hurt his value to his teams, but those home runs kept him in the majors for a sixteen-year career.

Whether "good pitching beats good hitting" or not—and you can find a fan to take either side of that argument any time—it's clear that good hitting has its value, even, so it appears, when the only thing a hitter can hit is 35 home runs a year. But there are lots of other ways to hit, and many other ways to score runs. Whatever strategies a manager uses on offense, whether he's stealing bases, ordering sacrifice bunts, signaling for a hit-and-run— whatever he does—it all has only one goal: score runs. It's the only way to win ball games, and any offensive move that doesn't contribute in some way to scoring runs is the wrong move.

GETTING ON BASE

You get up there, wait for the pitch, swing as hard as you can, and run like hell, right? Well, not exactly. There are a few things a major leaguer has to consider, and a major league fan might want to consider them as well. First, there are different kinds of hitters. Tony Gwynn, who plays for San Diego, is almost the exact opposite of Dave Kingman. He has won five National League batting titles and has a lifetime average of around .330. But he hits about 5 home runs a year and typically produces only about 60 runs batted in (although in the 1995 season he garnered over 90 RBIs). Remember: The point here is to score runs. No matter how good a batter's average is, if he isn't causing runs to cross the plate he's not doing the team any good. Dave Kingman, in that awe-inspiring year with the Mets when he hit .204, nevertheless pushed 99 runs across the plate. So who's a better hitter? Kingman made out 70 percent of the time; Gwynn makes out only 60 percent. Maybe Kingman did more good for the team, but Gwynn does less harm. That's got to be worth something.

But let's not get distracted now; we'll save discussions of such arcana for Chapter 5. For now, let's talk hitting.

Sometimes a batter will want an umpire to move—he's in his line of vision, distracting him from concentrating on the pitcher, standing in the batter's unlucky spot, whatever. The umpire doesn't have to move, but most will comply if asked nicely. And there's a sign for asking, nowhere encoded in the rules. The batter steps out of the batter's box, looks straight at the umpire he wants out of his way, and taps the top of his helmet, usually twice. We don't know where this comes from, but there it is.

Hitters are all alone, with no one to blame, and no one to take the credit, but themselves. Failure is the usual result of their efforts: The best hitters fail to get a hit about 70 percent of the time; worse hitters somewhat more often. Even if they do everything right— place their feet, rotate their hips, keep their heads down and their eyes on the ball, time their swings perfectly, and make a solid connection that sends the ball flying—even then, the result is usually an out. Tiny adjustments and improvements are all even the best hitters can hope for. The difference between batting .230 and batting .320 is only about two hits a week over a six-month season. Yet these two hits are the difference between a feared hitter and an easy out.

What is a hitter trying to do when he gets up to bat? The obvious answer would be: Avoid making an out. But the obvious answer is incorrect; he should be trying to help his team score a run. There are certain circumstances when the hitter is not trying to avoid making an out, but deliberately making out in a particular way in order to move a runner ahead of him further along the bases. This is called a *sacrifice*, and it can be done in several ways, depending upon the situation.

Suppose that it's the bottom of the ninth inning, tie score; your team has one out and a man on third. To win the game, all you have to do is get the runner on third home. It doesn't matter whether the hitter makes an out—if the runner on third crosses the plate, the game is over, and you've won. In a situation like this, the hitter is not thinking, *I have to get a hit and avoid making out.* He's thinking, *I have to get the ball somewhere that gives the player on third enough time to score—whether I make an out or not. All I have to do is get the ball out of the infield, and I'm the hero.* This is an example of a situation in which the hitter's intentions will have nothing to do with avoiding making an out.

THE NEXT GUY'S GONNA BUNT—TRUST ME

There are, of course, many more complicated situations in which making an out is not the worst thing to happen to the hitter. Although there is some debate about its value, most managers use the sacrifice bunt to move a runner safely from first to second (or sometimes second to third). The principle is simple: You tell your hitter to bunt—to hit the ball very softly in a way that will probably result in his making out but will at the same time move the runner from first to second, where, as you recall from Chapter 2, he is much more likely to score. You've sacrificed the batter for the greater good of the team—or at least that's the idea.

The anticipation of a sacrifice bunt is one of the great moments in any baseball game. Here you have everyone on the field and in the rival dugouts thinking at once. Sometimes a batter will try to conceal the fact that he's going to bunt. Just as often, everyone will know the bunt is coming, and there's no need to pretend. The offense is figuring out ways to make the bunt succeed; the defense is busy planning to defeat the strategy. The man on first is trying to stretch his lead. The pitcher is throwing over to first to try to keep him close to the bag and planning to throw the pitches that are hardest to bunt—high fastballs and curveballs away from the batter. The batter is ready to tap the ball and take off like a shot. And you get to watch it all play out—provided that you're paying close attention and prepared to enjoy the moment.

How can you know when the moment is coming? First and most obviously, there can be no sacrifice bunt if there are two out—you've got nothing left to sacrifice. Probably the two most common bunting situations are a runner on first with less than two outs and runners on first and second with nobody out. Remember: The point is to move runners into scoring position—but at the cost of one out. With a runner on first, you have to get him over to second if you want him to score. So even if you already have one out, it's probably worth a shot. When you get him to second, all you need is one base hit to score a run. On the other hand, with runners at first and second, you've already got a man in scoring position. If you already have one out, now's the time to get a hit, not a sacrifice. With runners on first and second and no one out, however, you can use a bunt to move two runners into scoring position and still have only one man out. Some managers like to sacrifice bunt early in the game, but most consider it a rather conservative move best saved for late innings. Usually bunts are more common in close games; if your team is substantially behind, a sacrifice isn't going to do you much good. If you only need a run to win, on the other hand, a sacrifice may be a good idea. So the later the inning and the closer the score, the more likely the bunt becomes. Understand that these are general rules only. Some managers love to sacrifice; others hate it. Orioles manager Davey Johnson, for example, almost never uses it. And even managers who like it will rarely use it before the seventh inning. There is even some argument based on statistical analysis about whether the sacrifice bunt is a good idea under any circumstances. But there's no argument at all about the fact that bunts are fun to watch. Here's how to watch them.

If a batter is told to bunt—and we'll get into how this command is delivered to him later—he has to be thinking about where and how he wants to bunt. His primary intention, remember, is not to get to first base safely himself—although he certainly wouldn't mind doing so—but to make it impossible for the infielders to throw out the guy heading for second. Where does he want to bunt? It depends on the situation.

Let's say you're at Yankee Stadium watching the Yankees playing Chicago. The White Sox have a man on first base, nobody out. It's late in the game, and the score is 1–0 Yankees. The guy coming up to bat is Ozzie Guillen, a light-hitting shortstop. Now's the moment—even before Guillen stands in the batter's box—to lean over to the person sitting next to you and say confidently, "This guy's going to bunt, and he's going to try to make the pitcher field it."

This truly easy way to impress people is yours free with this book. Here's why it will happen exactly the way you said it would: Guillen hits about .260 and has no power. So the manager isn't going to count on him to get a hit, or even to be able to get the ball out of the infield. He'll want him to sacrifice. Now Don Mattingly, a lefty, is playing first. You don't want him to field the ball, because a lefty swooping in on a bunt will have a good chance at a quick underhand throw to second. And Mattingly is a Gold Glove fielder, so you know he's going to do it right. You don't want Wade Boggs at third to get it either—he's a righty, also a Gold Glover, and he's perfectly built to make the mirror image of Mattingly's play, again nailing the runner at second. If either of these guys rushes in and grabs it, your sacrifice is going to turn into a fielder's choice, and you're going to be standing on first with two out—or worse, you'll be out on a double play, and the inning will be over. No, the person you want to field this bunt is the pitcher—he'll take extra time getting off the mound, and he'll likely have no time left to make an awkward 180-degree turn and throw to second. His only play will be to get you at first, which is exactly what you want. So Guillen will try to lay down the bunt in a place where only the pitcher can get to it.

> *"I've got nothing against the bunt—in its place. But most of the time that place is at the bottom of a long-forgotten closet."*
> —Earl Weaver

Now if Guillen had been facing a team with a right-handed first baseman, he would want that man to field the ball. A right-handed first baseman will likely have a difficult throw to second and have to resort to tossing the ball to the pitcher covering first. Again, the objective is accomplished: You've got your man over to second. With runners on first and second, whether the first baseman is a righty or a lefty, Guillen would like to see the third baseman field the ball: That pulls him off the base and puts him in an awkward position to try to spin around and throw to get the runner at third base (where, of course, the shortstop is covering). So in that situation, Guillen will aim his bunt down the third base line to make Boggs come in and get it. Man on second? Bunt the ball toward the right side of the infield; any decent bunt there will get the runner over to third and in position to score.

Of course, nothing is guaranteed. A good infield can turn even a well-placed sacrifice bunt into a double play. And some managers just don't like to give up the out in any case. Whatever else can be said about it, it costs you one of your 27 outs; so it's expensive. But there are other kinds of bunts for people who don't care to sacrifice.

Bunts for Those Who Just Won't Sacrifice

First, you can bunt for a base hit. There doesn't have to be anyone on base, and it doesn't have to be a game situation that demands a sacrifice. If a hitter is fast, if he's a good bunter, if the infielders are playing a little too deep, it may be the right moment to try to get a single by laying down a bunt. At lower levels, teams will try to bunt to weak infielders. In the majors, there aren't any infielders weak enough for this to work. But you can find even major league infielders playing too deep, and that can be a chance to bunt your way on. There are, however, pitchers who are weak fielders or whose pitching motions leave them in awkward postures for fielding, and a bunt plopped down in front of one of them can be a ticket to first base. Sometimes a hitter will try a bunt on wet grass, which can make the ball stop dead far away from any infielder's grasping hands. This doesn't work in indoor stadiums on plastic grass (and it's not the only thing you'll miss if you have to watch baseball in one of those places).

When a batter, especially a lefty, is bunting for a base hit, you'll often see him *drag bunt*. This means he starts running as he bunts the ball, apparently "dragging" it as he runs. Whereas a hitter bunting for a sacrifice doesn't really have to conceal his intentions, a hitter bunting for a base hit does. So he won't "square around" into the bunting position until the last possible second. A bunt for a base hit is best when put down the third base line—that makes the throw to first the longest. He may want to bunt down the first base line—past the pitcher—if the first baseman is playing particularly deep. A right-handed hitter will sometimes "push" a bunt toward the hole between first and second. But he'll avoid bunting toward the pitcher, which is the easiest way to make out.

The *suicide squeeze* is both vividly and aptly named. This is a desperate measure taken when it is absolutely essential to score a runner from third. On this play, the runner on third breaks for home with the pitch, and the hitter must bunt the ball on the ground. When it works, there's no defense against it: Almost simultaneously, the ball is bunted and the runner slides into the plate. If the batter misses the pitch, or pops it up, well, that's where the suicide part comes in. The runner is usually a dead duck. This is a very rare play. The fact is that it's easy to score a man from third in any case; you don't have to be so dramatic about it. It would only be used in special circumstances: a very close game in the late innings, one man out, weak hitter at the plate, and a count on the batter—1–0 or 2–0, for example—that requires that the pitcher throw a strike. Why not use it with nobody out? Because it's so easy to score from third with nobody out that it isn't worth sacrificing to do it. The safety squeeze is a variation of this—the runner checks to see if the bunt has been put down properly, and then decides himself whether to go home. This requires a man on third who has speed and judgment. The suicide squeeze, on the other hand, requires only blind obedience. Still, it's an exciting play on those rare occasions when you get to see one. If you do get to see one, afterward tell the story repeatedly and remind everyone that you were right there in the stadium at the time. Always add the details to make sure that everyone understands that it was a true suicide squeeze and not the safety squeeze variation. They'll claim to be bored with your story; you'll know they're just jealous.

A hitter can fake a bunt, and then take a short chop at the ball to send it past a charging infielder. This is used in one of those situations when the infielders are clearly expecting a bunt and charging in with the pitch. The batter turns to bunt, not trying to conceal his intentions. If he sees the infielders running in, he pulls his bat back from the bunting position and tries to slash the ball past them. This is called the *fake bunt and slash*. Charging infielders risk life and limb on the play, but few batters can successfully execute the move.

THE HIT-AND-RUN

Yes—you already know that when you hit, you have to run, and anyone on base has to run, too. But the hit-and-run is a little different. Here, the runner (or runners) and the batter are told—by signals from the third base coach—that the next pitch will be a hit-and-run. This means that as soon as the pitcher indicates that he is throwing to the plate, the runners start running, and whatever pitch is thrown, the batter must swing at it and hit it on the ground. This allows a runner on first who is not particularly fast to stay out of the double play. It requires a batter who can get his bat on the ball no matter where it's pitched and hit the ball on the ground—ideally, hitting it to the right side of the field to allow the runner on first to go to second, or a runner on second to third.

This is not a steal, so the runner doesn't have to take a big lead. In fact, if a runner gets picked off when a hit-and-run is on, he'd better have a pretty good excuse for it. Claiming severe injury or intervention by supernatural powers might work, but many managers would find even those excuses inadequate. There are other risks, of course. If the batter hits a line drive right at an infielder, it's going to be a double play, and there's nothing anyone can do about it. If the batter swings and misses, all the runner can do is try to complete the steal. When it works, it's an elegant piece of offense and even has some possible extra benefits: If there's a wild pitch, the runner can usually go to third; on a long single he might go all the way around to score.

When is a manager likely to resort to this play? When there are less than two out, a player with good bat control is at the plate who is ahead in the count, and his team is ahead, tied, or behind by one run. You're trying to get the runner over to second, and there are several ways to do it—sacrifice bunt, steal, wait for a hit. But the hit-and-run, which may be the riskiest way to do it, also has the most potential benefits. Look for this play late in the game. If you're behind by more than a run, you want the batter to get on base, too, and you don't want him swinging at anything except the perfect pitch. The hit-and-run is also effective with men on first and second, or men on first and third. The count on the batter is a big factor. Obviously, there's no hit-and-run when there are two strikes on the batter—it doesn't make sense to make a batter swing at a pitch when he could wind up striking out on it. You want a count where the pitcher is more or less obliged to throw a strike: first pitch, 1–0, 2–0, 2–1. If the batter has three balls on him, it's better to wait for a walk than to risk forcing a batter to swing at ball four. And on 3–0 and 3–1, you want the batter to take a big swing—not a little bat-control chop.

For the fan, this is a good one to try to anticipate. Look for the right situation (man on first, nobody out, no count on the batter, close score); make sure that all the elements are there. The guy next to you, who thinks he's smart, says, "I'll bet this is going to be a hit-and-run." "Nah," you say, in perfect baseballese. "Not on the first pitch. Pitcher's expecting it, so he'll bust him inside with a high fastball that he can't get to. Let that one go. Then, when the count is 1–0 and he has to throw a strike—that's the time to start this guy." Every once in a while, you'll be right.

STEALING BASES

> *"When we played softball, I'd steal second, then feel guilty and go back."*
> —WOODY ALLEN

Outright theft is one good way to advance the runner. Most players will wait for a sign from the third base coach telling them to steal at a given moment. The best base stealers in the majors—Rickey Henderson, Kenny Lofton, Vince Coleman, and others—usually are allowed to steal whenever they want. For guys like this, managers usually have a sign that says "Don't steal." You have to succeed about two-thirds of the time to do your team more good than harm when stealing. Henderson succeeds about 8 times in 10. Some say that stealing third is easier than stealing second, possibly because a runner can take a bigger lead from second than from first because the second baseman doesn't hold the runner on the bag. But that 127-foot throw from home to second past a 6-foot pitcher standing on a mound 10 inches high—well, try standing in back of home plate on a regulation baseball field and just look where the ball has to go. And it has to get there in under two seconds if you hope to catch someone. Anyway, if a base runner can succeed as often as Henderson does, he does his team a favor by taking off for second as often as possible.

How come it's so easy to steal second? If a fast runner takes a 15-foot lead off first, he can make it to second in 3.5 seconds. So that's how long the pitcher and catcher have to get the ball to second base. Pitchers take one second to go through their motion, and the ball takes about .4 seconds to reach the catcher's mitt. The best major league catchers can deliver the ball to second within two seconds after it hits the catcher's mitt—what coaches call the *pop-to-pop time*: pop! into the catcher's mitt; pop! into the shortstop or second baseman's mitt. Total: 3.4 seconds—when everything is done perfectly. That one-tenth of a second is the margin for error. This is good arithmetic for runners, but not so hot for the defense.

So for the defense, the best thing to do is to try to change the one variable in the equation that can be changed most radically:

Davey Lopes of the Dodgers stealing second base. The Houston second baseman seems to be begging for the ball, but it's too late. Lopes is safe again. *National Baseball Library & Archive, Cooperstown, NY*

> *"Today, I'm the greatest of all time."*
> —RICKEY HENDERSON, UPON BREAKING LOU BROCK'S LIFETIME STOLEN BASES RECORD. MADE DOUBLY IRRITATING BY THE FACT THAT HENDERSON WAS RIGHT: HE'D NOT ONLY STOLEN MORE BASES THAN BROCK, BUT HE'D BEEN SUCCESSFUL 81.3 PERCENT OF THE TIME AS OPPOSED TO BROCK'S 75.3 PERCENT.

reduce that 15-foot lead the runner is taking. Pitchers do this by throwing the ball over to first. Many pitchers do it a lot, and some fans get impatient to the point of rudeness when this happens. But throwing over really does make it more difficult to steal. The tolerances are very tight here—making a runner stand one foot closer to first before he starts for second can make all the difference. Some baseball experts have expressed doubts about the value of throwing to first—they say it distracts the pitcher from his primary job, doesn't really prevent people from stealing anyway, rarely results in a pickoff, and of course bores the fans silly. So some other baseball expert took the trouble to count how many times pitchers throw to first and correlate it with how many times runners try to steal on them. He counted 23,905 throws to first in 1990 and 4,800 stolen base attempts. In 1991, he counted 25,044 throws to first and 4,687 stolen base attempts. The stealing success rate was lower when there were more throws to first—68.5 percent of attempts were successful in 1990; only 66.6 percent were successful in 1991. This proves two things: First, you can find some fan somewhere willing to count almost anything; and second, throwing to first a lot does what you'd expect it to do—it helps keep people from stealing on you. So the next time you're at the stadium and someone next to you starts to boo loudly because the pitcher keeps throwing over to first, remind him firmly of this fact. No—on second thought, just keep it to yourself.

It's easier to steal second when there's a left-handed batter at the plate. He's standing right in the way of a right-handed catcher's throw, and the catcher will have to avoid him, which takes extra time. For the same reason, it's easier to steal third when there's a righty at bat. Expect a steal when the score is close or tied. When you're behind by more than one run, it's probably more important to get the batter on base than to move the runner over to second on a steal; if you're ahead by more than one run, there's no reason to take risks. On the other hand, with a base runner like Henderson, you can expect a steal almost every time he gets on base.

Watch a runner when he takes off for second. If he's doing it right, he'll take a quick glance down toward the batter after his second or third step; he wants to know what happened to the ball, because it may change his plans. There are several possibilities. A pop fly would make the runner stop and get ready to head back to first. A ground ball may result in a double play, so he'll want to be prepared to slide hard into the man covering second to try to break

Jackie Robinson Steals Home

Home, of course, is the hardest base of all to steal. The pitcher has the ball in his hand, and he's throwing it toward the plate in any case. To steal home, you need a tremendous jump, great speed, and a pitcher who takes a big, time-consuming windup. Perhaps the most spectacular steal of home in all of baseball history occurred in the first game of the 1955 World Series, when Jackie Robinson stole home in the eighth inning with Whitey Ford on the mound. Although the Dodgers wound up losing the game anyway, the steal has become legendary. So we hesitate, but we're going to say it: The umpire blew the call when he said that Robinson was safe. We've watched the film of that play, played it back and forth, stopped the action and started it again, and we're telling you, Berra had him. No Dodgers fan will believe us, and we're sorry ourselves to have to say it, but the man was out.

it up. If there's a base hit, he'll have to be prepared to go to third. He doesn't want to slide into second and stand there dusting himself off when he could be standing on third base. Same for a wild pitch or a passed ball—he'll want to see if he can make it to third after stealing second. If a runner doesn't look, he can wind up embarrassed. For example, an alert infielder can trick the runner into thinking that there's a play at second, even though the ball has been popped up: He runs over to the base as if to receive the ball, while one of the other infielders catches the pop-up. It is humiliating for a runner to slide into second in a cloud of dust, only to learn that the ball has been caught on a fly and he is out at first on a double play. Base runners, it is clear, have to think, run, and chew tobacco all at the same time.

> *"90 percent of this game is half mental."*
> —YOGI BERRA

The Double Steal

When a team has runners on first and third, it's time to start giving the defense a hard time. One way to do this is the double steal. Picture it: The runner on first takes off for second after the pitch is thrown. What's the catcher supposed to do? Throw to second to get him and let the guy on third score? Hold the ball to prevent the guy on third from scoring and let the runner move into scoring position without even trying to get him out? For the offense, even if the double steal doesn't score a run, it moves an extra runner into scoring position. And if it's done with only one out, it eliminates the possibility of a double play. You probably wouldn't want to do it with nobody out—no point in taking a risk when you could have a big inning brewing. But with one out, and especially with two out, it's a great play.

You can see several variations of the play. With one out, the runner from first will be trying to steal second, going in as hard as he can. With two outs, the object is to score the runner, so the man stealing second—if he doesn't actually succeed in getting there—has to get himself caught in a rundown long enough to allow the runner from third to score. If he gets tagged out before the run scores, the inning is over, and his team is out of luck. Usually, the runner on third will wait until the catcher throws the ball to second, and then take off. If the catcher doesn't throw, no problem; he'll just stay on third. Sometimes the man on first will take a ridiculously long lead, daring the pitcher to pick him off. If the pitcher throws over to the first baseman, he takes off for second as fast as possible. In the meantime, the man on third (remember him?) increases his lead and gets ready; as soon as the first baseman throws to second, he heads home. If the first baseman doesn't throw to second, he dashes back to third, and his team winds up with men at second and third.

There are even some trickier variations, designed to fool infielders. Here's one: The man on first waits for the pitcher to deliver the pitch, and then takes two big steps toward second. This makes the shortstop (or second baseman) look at him, but then realize that he's not stealing, so he doesn't cover the base. Then as soon as the pitch hits the catcher's mitt, the runner takes off for second. Surprise! No one is covering the base, so the catcher has to hold the ball, or he hesitates and then makes a bad throw. As soon as he does throw, the runner on third runs home to score. Here's another: You have a capable base stealer on first, so you tell him to steal second. When the catcher throws, the man on third fakes a break to home plate. The player covering second sees the break and fires the ball home without bothering to tag the runner sliding into second. Everybody's safe. (Note that infielders already know about these tricks and have their own ideas on how to respond.)

Whenever there are men on first and third, start thinking about what can happen. Especially with one or two out, something almost certainly will. This is one of those moments to be paying full attention—you can look around for another beer later. Get your head in the game now and watch some interesting things develop.

BASERUNNING

Speed is required, but it's not enough. Like almost everything else in baseball, if you want to run the bases right, you have to know something, and you have to be thinking. The first thing a baserunner has to remember is that he shouldn't be taking chances when his team is behind by two runs or more. It's hard enough to get on base—you don't want to give up an out by making risky moves on the base paths. So when should a runner try for an extra base or try to stretch a single into a double, or a double into a triple? Advice given to base runners by managers is (or should be) based on the probability of scoring.

One of the oft-repeated rules of baserunning is: Never make the first or third out at third base. If you have no one out, there's plenty of time to get to third—don't risk getting thrown out trying to stretch a double into a triple. And if you have two outs, it isn't worth it to risk it either: The increased probability of scoring from third with two outs as against scoring from second with two outs just doesn't make the gamble worth it. The best time to gamble on making it to third is with one out. With one out, standing on third is almost a guarantee of scoring a run, and that makes it a bet you want to take. The same logic applies when considering stretching a single to make it to second: The best time to do it is with two out. A two-out steal of second or a two-out single stretched to a double is a good play. With only one out left anyway, your chances of scoring from first are not good. You increase them tremendously if you make it to second. So go for it. The same kind of reasoning goes when a runner considers trying to score. With no one out, he'll only go home if he's absolutely sure he'll make it. With one out, he'll take a chance. With two out, he'll take an even bigger chance. With two out, for example, there's less than a 30 percent chance of being driven in with a base hit. So the runner might as well risk it. Running like a lunatic, Pete Rose style, is not necessarily the best approach, however good it makes you look when you succeed. It's better to know the odds and play them correctly.

Every Little Leaguer knows about tagging up. With less than two out, when a fly ball is hit, you hold your foot on the base until the ball is caught. Then you can run for the next base. But by the time you get to the majors you've learned that you shouldn't always stand on the base and wait. First, in the majors you can almost never make it from first to second on a fly out, no matter how deep the ball is hit. So a man on first will never stand on the base. Instead he'll go partway to second—closer to second if the ball is hit to left field, not so close if it's hit to right—and wait there until it's caught. Then he'll run back to first. If it isn't caught, he's practically at second base and may contemplate third. If he's starting on second, he may tag up, or he may not, depending on how many are out. With nobody out he'll wait right on second. If the ball is caught, he'll advance to third, with a good chance to score since now there's only one out. If the ball falls for a hit, he'll make it to third anyway and may even go all the way home. But with one out, the runner will go halfway to third—if the ball is caught, he retreats to second. If it drops in for a hit, he scores easily. This is because with two out, it doesn't matter that much whether he's on second or third—you'll probably need a base hit to score from either place. But with one out, being on third is a big advantage over being on second; you can score even without a base hit.

MOVING THE RUNNER ALONG

This much is clear: You have to touch all the bases before you score, so moving runners along from one base to the other is the only way to score runs. Stealing, taking the extra base, stretching a single into a double or a double into a triple, these are the ways teams score runs—unless they have someone who can belt the ball out of the park on a regular basis. So managers and players spend a good deal of time thinking about when to run and when not to run.

In general, teams are conservative when they're behind by two or more runs. This is perfectly logical: If you need to score two runs just to get even, getting only the lead runner home won't help you. You have to get the guy behind him home, too. So in situations like this, teams will not take chances. When the game is close or tied or when you're ahead, then it's time to take some risks. With two out, for example, you'll want to steal second, or try to stretch a single into a double. If you only have one out, you'll try to steal third or stretch a double into a triple. Same for trying to make it home: If you've made it to third with two outs, it's worth a gamble to try for the plate.

With men on first and third and less than two outs, you'll always see a runner on third try to score on a grounder to the infield. If he gets caught, he'll try to get himself in a rundown long enough to allow the runner from first to make it to third and the batter to make it to second.

Suppose there's a man on third with one out. The infield is playing in, to try to catch him if he heads for the plate. What should the runner do if the batter hits a grounder? He could stay on third and let the runner get thrown out at first. But then there would be two outs, and scoring from third with two outs usually requires a base hit. So if his team is ahead, or the score is tied, or he's only one run behind, he should head home. That's the percentage play, even with the infield in and ready to try to nail him at the plate. On the other hand, if there are none out, it's better to wait to make sure that the grounder goes through before heading home. If it doesn't and if the batter is thrown out, you still have another chance from third with one out.

So it's all quite logical: You take chances when you have to, and you don't when the percentages say not to. The attentive fan can anticipate what's going to happen by thinking about the score, what inning it is, how many runners are on which bases, and how many are out.

BATTING ORDER

Much thought is given to what order batters hit in. There are individual tastes in these matters, but certain general rules apply. The first man up—the leadoff batter—is usually a fast runner who can make good contact with the ball. He usually doesn't have much power; instead, he has a high on-base average. He hits a lot of singles and walks a lot, and the best leadoff hitters are almost always a threat to steal. The second man up is also a good contact hitter—he'll be the one to start the hit-and-run. He'll be asked to take a pitch now and then to give the leadoff man time to steal. He should be a good bunter and prepared to sacrifice when called upon. The third, fourth, and fifth batters are often referred to as "the heart of the order." These are the power hitters whose job it is to knock in runs. These guys hit a lot of homers—and they often strike out a lot, too. The sixth man is usually fast and a good contact hitter. The man in the seventh slot should be good at getting his bat on the ball for the hit-and-run. Eighth and ninth are reserved for the weakest hitters; you want them up as little as possible over the course of the season, so you put them down at the bottom of the order. In the National League, where pitchers still come up to bat, the pitcher bats ninth.

Where a man bats in the order can drastically affect his success as a hitter. For example, in 1961, when Roger Maris hit 61 homers, he was never walked intentionally. Not once. If he had been, maybe one or two or three of those homers would never have been hit. The reason he was never walked intentionally is that the person up next was Mickey Mantle. No manager in his right mind would deliberately put people on base for Mantle to drive in. Probably the best place to bat, if you want to get pitches that are easy to hit, is after a guy who steals a lot of bases and before a power hitter. With a man on base threatening to steal, the pitcher will hesitate to throw you curveballs—they allow the base stealer that much more time. And he won't want to walk you because that puts another runner on for the power hitter. So if you're lucky enough to wind up in such a position in the lineup, you can count on fastballs over the plate—the pitcher really has no other choice. That makes hitting a lot easier.

It's always fun to argue about where in the order a batter should be hitting. Usually, these arguments center on the "heart of the order" hitters. If a star power hitter gets into a slump, you can loudly insist that he be moved from third to fifth in the batting order. Some will argue that this is no way to treat a star player, that moving him will be demoralizing and embarrassing, that it's just not right to treat a guy this way when he's done so much for you. But stick to your guns: "If you're not producing, you shouldn't be batting third" is one good way to put it. Holding this opinion and expressing it courageously is solid proof that you know what you're talking about, and, even more important, that you're no weak-minded sentimentalist.

SIGNS AND SIGNALS

With all the stuff that can go on when there are men on base, a manager has to have a way to tell his players what he wants them to do and to make sure that everyone has the same thing in mind. You've seen the third base coach wipe his hand across his chest, clap his hands twice, touch the visor of his cap, take it off, put it back on, rub first his left sleeve, then his right, scratch his ear, rub his nose, stand up straight, and put his hands on his knees. And you'll notice, if you watch closely, that the batter is standing outside the batter's box staring at this pantomime with immense interest and concentration. It's not that he's amused; he's learning what he's supposed to do on the next pitch by watching the signs.

In general, major league teams have about a half dozen signs that get flashed between the third base coach and his hitters and runners (we're not talking here about catcher's signs to the pitcher or the signs exchanged by the second baseman and shortstop, which are discussed elsewhere). There are signs for take the pitch, hit-and-run, steal, double steal, fake bunt and slash, the squeeze bunt, and the sacrifice bunt. The point of it all is to prevent the other team from understanding what the signs mean; but the ways they can be designed and delivered are, theoretically, infinite. You can devise a simple system with four or five signs, each meaning something different, or you can devise a system so complicated that you can wind up hiding it not only from the other team but from your own as well.

The basic method is fairly simple. A team might work it out something like this: Touching the hat means hit-and-run; touching the waist means a bunt; touching the cheek means take the pitch, and so on. Then there's an indicator sign—the sign that means that "the next sign I give you is the one you must pay attention to." So the third base coach can go through whatever gyrations he wants to until he shows the indicator sign—touching his left elbow with his right hand, for example. Then the batter or runner knows that the next sign is the one that counts. The coach will face the batter when he's communicating with him, and the runners when he wants to sign to them. Usually, a runner and a hitter each have a sign that means "I got the sign, and I know what you're telling me to do." These are subtle gestures—holding fingers next to the thigh in a certain way, readjusting some piece of equipment, and so on. There's even a sign that a player can give to the coach that means "Go through the signs again. I didn't get it the first time." For some reason, this is the same on every team: The player rubs his hand across the letters on the front of his shirt.

George Will tells the story of the young Yogi Berra, who, every time he got on base, would jabber away with the first baseman—until he got the hit-and-run sign. Then he'd fall into pensive silence. Other teams noticed this, and he started to get picked off more and more often. First, his coaches told him to shut up. Then realizing that with Yogi this was hopeless, they told him to just keep on talking.

Of course, you don't have to make it simple, and in fact at the major league level, some managers can make it pretty complicated.

You can have two indicator signs; you can divide the body into four quarters, with touches to each quarter meaning something different; you can devise signs to tell runners to take long leads, to run on a pickoff or dive back to the base, to pull a delayed steal. You can direct hitters not only to bunt, or to hit away, but also to fake a bunt and then hit away. The reason you'd want to make signs complicated is not only because major league players have the skills to do more, but also because the other team is trying to decode them, and this must be prevented.

The first line of defense against sign stealing is the player: He has to be careful not to make some unconscious gesture that gives away the *hot sign*—the sign among all the irrelevant gestures that means something. Widening your eyes, slapping your forehead, or doing a double-take every time you see the hot sign is certainly not considered good form, but inexperienced players at levels below the majors can be almost that obvious about it. They'll do all sorts of things to let everyone on the field know which sign was the important one—nod, turn away from the coach, hitch their pants, or grip the bat in characteristic ways. Major leaguers don't make such obvious mistakes, but they're certainly capable of missing signs—especially when paranoid coaches and managers devise systems so complicated that they fool their own players.

Watch the third base coach in a situation when there is likely to be a play on. He'll go through a remarkable variety of gestures while the batter and runners stare at him. If you watch closely enough, you may be able to see the acknowledging sign from the player. Then on the next pitch, you'll see what it all meant. And the other team is watching closely, too, trying to figure out what the signs mean. To steal signs successfully, you usually need a couple of people cooperating with each other. Here's how it works.

Sitting in the dugout, the head thief will watch the third base coach (or the manager, if he is giving the signs). An accomplice will watch the batter or runner. When the batter or runner makes one of those unconscious gestures—looks away, hitches his pants, and so on—the man watching him shouts, "Stop." The man watching the coach takes note of what sign was given just before the "stop." That's the sign that counts—whatever happens on the next play, that was the sign for it. Now, of course, I've simplified things quite a bit, and the other team knows these methods too, so they're busy making sure that the method doesn't work. But that pretty well summarizes the science of stealing signs. The rest is art, and some people are much better at it than others.

One of the great sign stealers is Joe Nossek, a coach for various American League teams, most recently Chicago. He was a journey-man outfielder during a six-year playing career in the 1960s, but he really found his calling as a decoder of other teams' signs. There's no single key to Nossek's method. He'll watch a team's actions over several games to see its patterns. If he sees a team that hasn't done anything in the way of stealing or hit-and-runs, and then suddenly he sees a whole new batch of signs coming down from third, he'll know something must be on. He also watches the man-ager and the third base coach closely and then, as he puts it, "things start falling into place." Sort of like staring at a crossword puzzle for fifteen minutes and then suddenly seeing nine or ten words pop right out at you. Nossek is good at crossword puzzles, too.

Sometimes stealing signs requires no tricks at all—just a wide-awake player with a good memory. Tom Petroff in his book *Baseball Signs and Signals* tells what happened in the fourth game of the 1952 World Series. The Dodgers were behind by one run with men on second and third when Dodger manager Charley Dressen gave the squeeze sign to pitcher Joe Black, the batter. Dressen, unfortu-nately, was a man of habit. He'd used the same squeeze sign when he managed in the minors with the Oakland team of the Pacific Coast League. One of his players on that team was Billy Martin—the second baseman now playing for the Yankees. Martin saw the sign, flashed it to the catcher, Yogi Berra, and Berra called for a pitch outside where Black couldn't reach it. The runner was out easily. Martin, of course, would later have a highly successful six-teen-year career as manager of the Yankees, the A's, and other teams. His talents were evident at an early age.

Striking Them Out Is the Best Revenge

We've talked a lot now about how to run the bases and move runners across the plate. But because a book is a linear narrative, we can only talk about one thing at a time. A baseball game, like most sports contests, is nonlinear: Everything is happening at once. There's another game going on while your team is batting: nine players trying to stop your guys from hitting, running, stealing, and scoring. In other words, the defense is constantly figuring out ways to spoil the best-laid plans of runners and hitters. For every strategy, tactic, or play that's been described, there's a corresponding defensive move designed to prevent it from succeeding.

Obviously, the best way the defense can prevent runners from advancing is to keep them off base in the first place: Simply have a pitcher who can get everyone out. This, of course, is unrealistic. One of the many charms of the game is that in baseball, as in life, nothing is perfect. There are no unscored-upon teams, no undefeated seasons. In normal years, even the best teams lose about a third of their games (and the worst teams win a third). The team many consider the best ever, the 1927 Yankees, finished nineteen games ahead of the second-place Philadelphia Athletics; had a team batting average of .307; included in their lineup Babe Ruth, Lou Gehrig, and Earle Combs, all of whom hit over .350; and, in addition to hitting everything thrown at them, had a pitching staff with the lowest earned run average in the league. Even these Yankees managed to lose forty-four times during that season—more than 28 percent of the time. So damage will be done to any team, and teams can only hope to exercise good damage control. Let's see how they do it.

THE PITCHER PICKOFF

"I throw four wide ones, and then I try to pick him off first."
—PREACHER ROE, EXPLAINING HOW TO PITCH TO STAN MUSIAL

When a runner is thrown out while taking a lead off a base, he is said to be *picked off*. If you can't keep a batter off the bases, the next best thing is to pick him off after he gets there—throw the ball to one of the infielders and have him tag the runner out. Usually, the pitcher is the one to start the process, but he's very restricted in the ways he is allowed to throw. If his motions vary from the rules, he can be guilty of a balk—and the runner will get a free trip to the next base. (The balk is one of the most difficult infractions to spot in baseball. See Chapter 2 for the details.) So the pitcher moves his arms and legs very carefully when there's a man on base—not only to avoid balking, but also to minimize the time it takes to deliver the ball to the plate. He doesn't want to go into a big long windup before he throws, because this will give the runner on base more time to steal. He wants to deliver the ball in such a way as to make the runner think he can still throw over to first until the very last moment. This keeps the runner close to the base. Runners watch pitchers very carefully, learning the tiny idiosyncrasies of their motions to try to figure out when they're going to pitch, and when they're going to throw to first.

Watch a right-handed pitcher with a man on first. He brings his two hands to the "set" position—at his waist, with his hand in his glove holding the ball. He peeks over his left shoulder at the runner. He sees the runner taking a slightly larger lead, tensing up, ready to steal. He waits. He looks in toward the catcher again. He peeks over his shoulder once more at the runner. He looks back at the catcher one more time, and then suddenly steps toward first with his left foot and throws to the first baseman. The key here is that the pitcher must move his left foot toward first base when he throws there— if he moves it in any other direction, it's a balk, and the runner takes second for free.

A left-handed pitcher has some advantages over a righty: He's facing first base, and his normal leg lift before he pitches cannot be distinguished from a leg lift to throw to first—until he actually steps toward home or toward first. In other words, he can go into his normal pitching motion and then suddenly change it and throw to first instead of to the batter. In addition, the lefty has another option, the recently developed *flip move*. Here the lefty doesn't start his motion to the plate at all. Instead, he takes a quick step with his left foot back off the pitching rubber and then flips the ball with a very short arc of his arm to first. A pitcher has to have his foot on the rubber when he takes the sign from the catcher and comes to the set position; but when his foot is off the rubber, he's just another infielder, and he can throw to first any time and in any way he wants. So with a lefty, you're watching for two entirely different moves— one before he starts his motion to the plate, one after. He faces the same constraints as a righty as far as balking is concerned—if he steps toward the plate with his foot on the rubber and then throws to first, it's a balk, and the runner takes second.

The runner, in the meantime, is watching the pitcher's move. He's watched it before—probably even seen videotapes of it—and he notices everything. The slightest twitch can reveal whether the pitcher intends to throw over. The direction of the pitcher's shoulder, the angle of his knee or elbow, the way he holds his hands in the set position—any of these mannerisms may tip him off. Pitchers, naturally, try to minimize or conceal such mannerisms, or make them inconsistent with the actions that follow them.

If a runner does get picked off—that is, finds himself standing between first and second while the first baseman is holding the ball— he doesn't have much choice: He has to run for second in a desperate attempt to make it. Unless the first baseman completely blows it with a bad throw, the runner is surely out.

Runners can be picked off the other bases, too. A pickoff at second can be particularly elegant in its execution. Here, the pitcher has his back to the runner, so he needs help in telling him when to throw over. Often the catcher gives the signal—to both the pitcher and the man covering second—that the time is right. Simultaneously, the second baseman runs to cover second; the pitcher wheels around and throws; and, if all goes according to plan, the runner on second is caught. There are variations in the way this play can be executed. Sometimes the shortstop will take a few quick steps toward second, and then stop, trying to convince the runner that there is no throw coming. But while the runner is distracted looking at the shortstop, the second baseman sneaks up to cover the bag. The pitcher wheels and throws, catching the runner with his pants down. This requires careful signals between the shortstop, second baseman, pitcher, and sometimes the catcher; and it requires timing to make it all work exactly right. The pitcher doesn't look at the base before he throws—he counts two beats and then turns around and throws the ball. The second baseman, having counted the same two beats, is there to catch it. With a man on second, a pitcher—either a lefty or a righty—can lift his leg to begin his motion and then swing around and throw to second. Again, this requires a prearranged signal between the pitcher and the man covering second base, and it demands careful timing—the pitcher looks at second and throws at the same moment, so he has to know that someone will be covering.

One particularly graceful variation is sometimes called the *daylight play*. Here, the pitcher looks back toward second base and notices that the shortstop has inched over behind the runner so that he can see daylight between the runner and the shortstop to the runner's left. The pitcher and shortstop signal each other—sometimes even just eye contact is enough—and then the pitcher turns back to the plate. Pitcher and shortstop start counting silently, one, two, three as the shortstop moves toward second. On three, the pitcher wheels and throws. Bingo! No more man in scoring position.

A pitcher can't fake a throw to first base—that would be a balk. But the rules say that he can fake a throw to second or third. Although lots of fans scream "Balk!" when pitchers do this, it isn't a balk. Pitchers routinely do this to bluff runners back to third base, and sometimes to second base as well. Right-handed pitchers, because they are facing third base in their normal pitching position, are better at picking runners off third. This, too, is a play that must be arranged beforehand, in this case with a signal to the third baseman. The righty lifts his leg as if to pitch to the plate, then steps toward third and throws. The third baseman arrives at the base just in time to tag the runner out.

Defending Against the Steal

We discussed this a bit in Chapter 2, where we went over the jobs of the second baseman and the shortstop. One of these two players is almost always involved in preventing runners from stealing. The second baseman or the shortstop will take the throw from the catcher on the steal of second base, and they'll decide in consultation with each other on who covers the base to receive the throw. That's relatively simple. With two men on, though, things get complicated. The fielders—and the spectators—have much more to watch.

The typical double steal occurs with men on first and third. The pitcher winds up to pitch, and the runner on first breaks for second. Simultaneously, the runner on third runs for home. The catcher has to decide: Do I throw to second and risk letting a run score? Or do I throw to third to try to get that runner out? Or do I just hold the ball and prevent the run from scoring, but let the runner from first take second for free? Most managers would feel that the last choice is the worst. When a catcher chooses not to choose, well, existentially speaking, that's a choice too. And it's the wrong choice. It is not uncommon, even in the major leagues, to see a catcher concede second base to the runner in this way, figuratively shrugging his shoulders and tossing the ball back to the pitcher. But as a spectator and a fan, you shouldn't settle for this kind of behavior; and when it happens, it's best to complain loudly about incompetent catchers and infielders (try to avoid the phrases "these days" or "in my day"). The catcher should always make a play in this situation, and there are various factors he and his teammates must consider.

The basic move is to check to see what the runner at third is doing—he's more important than the man on first. If he's already broken for the plate, the catcher must throw to third and get the runner in a rundown so he can be tagged out. If he hasn't yet broken, there's probably time for a throw to second and then back to home to try for a double play. The third baseman can help by registering his opinion of the chances of getting the man out. Raising his hands in the air or shouting to the catcher are two means the third baseman may use to indicate that he would like the ball thrown to him. These decisions, of course, have to be made in split seconds, more by instinct and through experience than by intellect.

The pitcher can help, too. If the catcher decides to throw to second, the pitcher can pretend to catch the ball on the way—making the runner on third think that the pitcher has the ball will certainly discourage him from trying to run home. Now the second baseman (or the shortstop, if he is covering second base) enters the picture. He stations himself in such a way that he can throw home, throw to third, or tag the runner—a couple of feet in front of second base is a good place for him to stand and await the throw. At the last second, he decides what to do: tag the runner coming into second, throw to the catcher to get the runner at home, or throw to third to get the runner there.

The catcher has some other possibilities as well. He can fake a throw to second, make the runner from third think he can go home safely, and then catch him off base with a throw to the third baseman. Or he can throw the ball to second in such a way—low enough and directly over the pitcher's mound—that the pitcher can easily cut it off and fire it back home to get the runner that way. The pitcher is only 60 feet from home, whereas the second baseman is 127 feet away. Many teams have the second baseman cut off the throw well in front of second base—say, 80 or 90 feet from home. On this play, the runner on third heads for home as soon as he sees the ball pass the pitcher's mound, unaware that it isn't going all the way to second and that he therefore doesn't have as much time as he thinks he does.

Sometimes the purloined letter technique works: Do the obvious when the offense is expecting some fancy deception. For example, when the catcher sees the runner break for second base, he just fires to third with no questions asked. Occasionally, you find a runner who is thinking too much and just gets caught off base—the easy way.

Want to get tricky? Here's one: The manager, absolutely certain that the double steal is going to happen on the next pitch, calls for a pitchout. The shortstop runs over to cover second. The second baseman stations himself halfway between second and the pitcher's mound. When the catcher gets the ball on the pitchout, he holds it for a split second to keep the runner on third from breaking for home; then he throws toward second. The third baseman directs traffic: He yells if the runner starts to go home. If the runner on third doesn't break, the second baseman lets the throw go through to the shortstop covering second to tag the runner sliding in there. If the man on third breaks for home, the second baseman cuts off the throw and throws home. In the ideal (for the defense) situation, you get the guy sliding into second, and you've delayed the man on third long enough that you can still get him at home. Of course, when you get fancy like this, everything has to work perfectly. You have to know the double steal is on. The second baseman and the shortstop both run toward second base and leave gigantic holes on either side of the infield, so you have to make darn sure that the batter doesn't get his bat on the ball. The pitchout has to be perfect to allow the catcher to make his throw in time. And everyone in the infield has to be paying strict attention.

The double steal is a very entertaining play, and not uncommon. You can see it often enough to get some practice. Pretty soon, you'll be able to predict when one is coming—and offer a learned critique of the defense arrayed against it.

STOPPING THE HIT-AND-RUN

OK, we'll say it first: The best defense against the hit-and-run is not to let the batter hit the ball. Getting a strike on the batter and then throwing the runner out at second is, for the defense, just perfect. But, of course, throwing strikes is the best defense against everything. Because it isn't sensible to rely on this, there are other defenses devised to counter the hit-and-run.

Perhaps as obvious as throwing strikes is picking off the man on first. No runner on first, no hit-and-run. The pitcher's methods for doing this were discussed earlier, but the catcher can pick off runners too, and the best catchers throw often. Usually a catcher pickoff starts with a pitchout. On a signal from the catcher (sometimes from the manager), the pitcher throws the ball far outside where the batter can't reach it. This in itself is a defense against the hit-and-run: If the batter can't get his bat on the ball, there's no hit and therefore no hit-and-run. The pickoff from the catcher also requires that the infielders see the signal from the catcher that the pitchout is coming. They're then prepared, whether at first, second, or, more rarely, third base, to receive the throw. They'll move over to the base as late as possible to avoid telling the runner what's happening.

All major league ballplayers know when a hit-and-run is likely, so who are we kidding here? "On this first pitch," says the catcher to himself, "they're planning a hit-and-run. So I better call a pitchout. But they know that I think they're planning a hit-and-run, so they won't hit-and-run. But they know that I'm thinking that they're not going to hit-and-run, so they will. But they know that, too, so . . ." Catchers, like anyone else, can get in a lot of trouble if they think too much.

Of course, if your infield is good and the hit-and-run isn't executed quite properly, you can always hope for the double play anyway. But when a hit-and-run is properly executed, there's not much the defense can do about it except hope to get the sure out at first. The defense has to get going before the play begins. With pickoff attempts by the pitcher or catcher and the occasional well-timed pitchout, you can do a lot to disrupt the opposition's plans.

INFIELD POSITIONING

Sometimes you see the infielders playing way back on the outside edge of the infield; other times they're right in almost on the grass. Why? Because at different times, you're trying to accomplish different things. In a close game, with a man on third and less than two out, your priority is to stop the run from scoring. Remember, this guy can score on an infield grounder—unless you're playing in and are ready to make a fast throw to the plate. Of course, there's a downside to playing in: You limit the range of the infielders, and a sharp grounder is more likely to get through for a base hit.

Suppose, instead, that you're two runs ahead; it's the eighth inning; and there's a man on third with one out. Now where do you put your infielders? Think about it: Which player on the other team represents the most important out? That's right: the batter, because he's the tying run. It's much more important to get the batter for the second out than to risk letting a ball through the infield and having the tying run on first base with only one out. So here, the manager will tell his infield to play back, get the sure out at first, and let the run score. If you do that, it's bases empty, two out, and you're still one run ahead.

This is a good place to disagree with the manager. Not all managers will position the infield in the same way in a given situation. In fact, there are some compromisers who'll play the infield halfway, providing what some would say is the worst of both worlds. Form strong opinions about infield positioning and complain loudly when a team doesn't do exactly what you know they should. This can be especially satisfying when the infield is playing in, you tell everyone that they should be playing back, and the next pitch is hit just out of the reach of the pulled-in shortstop.

PREVENTING BUNTS FROM SUCCEEDING

Major leaguers know—and so do you now—when a sacrifice bunt is likely. It's late in the game; the score is close; you have less than two outs and runners are on first, first and second, or first and third. You've got a good bunter at bat and some speed on the base paths. Here's what to watch for.

Man on first. The pitcher gets ready to field the ball. He'll listen to the catcher for directions on whether to throw to second or first. The first and third basemen are charging in to field the ball if it

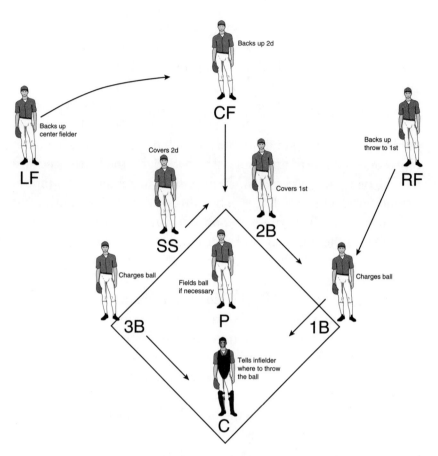

Defending against the bunt with a man on first.

comes their way. They, too, will listen for the catcher to tell them where to throw. The second baseman runs over to cover first base while the shortstop takes second base. The outfielders aren't idle either. The center fielder backs up the second baseman; the left fielder backs up the center fielder; and the right fielder backs up the first baseman. The third baseman will almost always field the bunt with his bare right hand, ready to throw underhand either to second or first. Same for the first baseman—no point in putting the ball into the glove first.

Men on first and second. Now it gets interesting. You could play it safe and keep it simple by just getting the man at first. In that

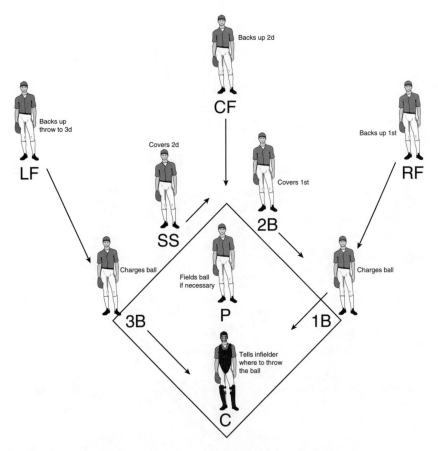

Backs up 2d

CF

Backs up
throw to 3d

Covers 2d

Backs up 1st

LF

Covers 1st

RF

SS

2B

Charges ball

Fields ball
if necessary

Charges ball

3B

P

1B

Tells infielder
where to throw
the ball

C

Defending against the bunt with men on first and second; getting the out at first.

case, the same things are going to happen as with a man on first only. The bunt will be fielded by the pitcher, first baseman, or third baseman. If the third baseman fields it, of course, there's no play at third. There still might be a play at second—again, the catcher directs traffic—but the main point is to make sure that you get the runner at first.

Of course, this is kind of giving up—you get the runner at first, but the sacrifice has succeeded. Short of coming up with a double play, what you really want to do is get the lead runner on the force play at third. To do that, teams use the *wheel play*. You'll know this is what's happening because just as the pitcher pitches, the shortstop

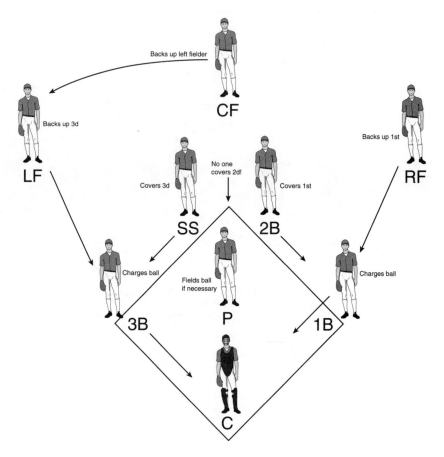

The wheel play. Defending against the bunt with men on first and second; getting the out at third.

breaks to cover third base—he has to beat the runner there, so he wants to start as soon as possible. The second baseman runs over to cover first. The first and third basemen charge in; the pitcher gets ready to field. The catcher shouts which base to throw to—third, if everything works as planned; first if it doesn't. The left fielder backs up third; the center fielder backs up the left fielder; the right fielder backs up first base. And everyone has to remember that, as you may have already noticed, *no one is covering second base*. So they can't throw there, even if the runner is the slowest guy in the league!

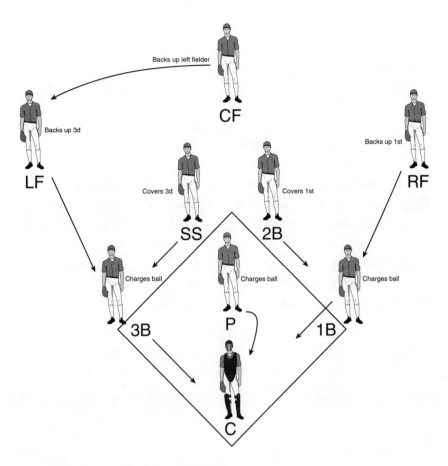

Defending against the squeeze bunt.

But there's a tricky variation of this, too. When the runner sees the shortstop break for third, he may assume that the wheel play is on, that the pitcher is going to throw to the plate, and that he'd better take off, too. But not so fast. The pitcher can still turn and throw to second, neatly picking him off. Watch the shortstop on this play—but never jump to conclusions. The first baseman can do a variation of this play, too. Before the pitch, he takes a couple of deliberate steps toward the plate, stops suddenly, and retreats back to the base to take the pickoff throw and catch the runner off guard.

Don't assume that a charging first baseman will keep charging. Watching the bunt defense, in full knowledge of all the possibilities, is thoroughly absorbing.

Man on third. The squeeze bunt, properly executed, is almost impossible to defend against. Remember that this play is rarely used; it would only come up when an essential run is on third that you need to cross the plate right now. The defense knows this, of course, so it plays well in, right on the edge of the grass. The third baseman, first baseman, and pitcher charge hard toward the plate in the hope that they can pick up the ball and shovel it home in time for a tag. The second baseman covers first in case there's a play on the batter; the shortstop covers third in case there's a rundown between third and home. Finally, the defense can hope that the batter will pop up the bunt instead of laying it on the ground. When this happens, there's a double play, and a memory that will last a lifetime.

You Could Look It Up: The Records

Gathering baseball statistics was once just newspaper reporting. Then it became a hobby, a preoccupation, an obsession, and, finally, an industry. At least two dozen books of statistics, half of them incomprehensible, are published every year. So why do we need a chapter on the records in a book like this? Here's why.

More than any other team sport, baseball is a game of recordable accomplishment. For most players on a football team, for example, there is little in the way of useful numbers to record. Once you get beyond pass completions, receptions, yards gained, and sacks—numbers that apply to a limited number of the eleven men on the team—there's not much left to write down. You have to watch an offensive tackle do his job to see if he's any good. There may be some statistics you can record to estimate what kind of player he is, but they wouldn't be useful unless you watched him play many times. In basketball, there are points, of course, and assists and blocked shots; and some clever statisticians have developed a few more categories from this raw material. But none of these efforts has produced anything like the volume of statistics that grows with every baseball season, and, probably more important, none of this data (or so it appears) has the predictive power of baseball's records.

If you could draw a graph of the baseball talent of all Americans (we're presuming here that you could find a single number to describe baseball talent), you'd probably wind up with one of those familiar bell-shaped curves. A small number of people would have no ability at all—can't throw, can't hit, can't run, can't do much of anything. Then a much larger number would fall in the middle of the curve. They can throw and hit, sort of, but they wouldn't be picked first when you're choosing up sides. Then moving toward the right-hand side of the curve, you'd find a smaller, but still significantly large number of people who can play—high school ball, let's say, or Babe Ruth League, or for a college team. An even smaller number would be good enough to play in the minor leagues—about 5,500 or so. Then when you get all the way over to the right, way down where the curve starts to disappear, you'd find Major League Baseball players. Only 700 or so people in the world at any one time are good enough to play in the majors, and all of them are very, very good at playing baseball. This means that the differences between them are tiny. All are excellent; a few are truly superb. Talent in the major leagues, unlike talent in the whole population, cannot be graphed on a bell-shaped curve. What you would have in our imaginary graph of talent in the majors is the very tip of the right-hand end of the curve: Everyone is top-notch.

So if everyone is excellent, how can you distinguish between, say, two major league hitters? How can you tell which one is really better? It wouldn't help to watch each of them take a turn at bat. I doubt that even the cleverest baseball scout in the world could tell the difference between a .260 hitter and a .320 hitter by watching each of them bat once. He'd be able to notice some things—body build, strength, bat speed, power of the swing, and so on—and the best scouts learn a lot this way about a young man's potential. But .320 hitters sometimes strike out, and .260 hitters sometimes hit home runs. So to make a really reliable prediction about what this player will do over a six-month season, the scout needs the records. He has to know what the guy did in his last 200, 300, even 1,000 times at bat before he can reliably say what he'll do in the future. But armed with all the information about what happened during those 1,000 times at bat, he'll be able to say quite a lot. Those statistics are important because they have great power to do something we all try to do in one way or another: predict the future.

> *"If a baseball statistic is meaningless to you, that's simply because you don't know what it means."*
> —BILL JAMES

The statistics don't predict everything, of course. There are plenty of stories of minor leaguers with great numbers whose careers never went anywhere. And there are enough tales of the superstar who wasn't picked until the fifteenth round of the amateur draft to make you wonder about the value of the stats (or the scouts). But most baseball people recognize the importance of statistics. They are used by managers to make hundreds of decisions about what players to use in given situations: How does this hitter do against lefties? What's his record against this particular pitcher? Does he hit well in stadiums with artificial turf? Is he better in night games than in day games? Better in enclosed stadiums than in the open air? How does he do with men on base? Of course, these numbers are also used by players to argue with owners about how much they should be paid, by owners to argue back, and by arbitrators to settle the arguments. And, most important for our purposes, they can be used by fans to learn what to expect from a player, what he will do for the team, and whether what he does is a routine baseball accomplishment or something truly extraordinary. Any fan who understands the meaning of getting 200 hits in a season, or 125 RBIs, or batting .300, or having an ERA of 2.75, or striking out 200 batters will understand more about what a given baseball player has accomplished and can be expected to accomplish in his next at bat or next time on the mound.

THIS IS FOR YOUR PERMANENT RECORD

Each league has an official statistician, appointed by the president of the league, whose job it is to maintain specific records, which the rule book delineates. Compared to the number of statistics that have been developed by baseball fans and "sabrmetricians" (from the acronym for the Society for American Baseball Research), there are actually very few percentage records recognized by Major League Baseball as "official," few enough to summarize them here easily:

1. Winning percentage for pitchers. Divide the number of games won by the total of games won and lost.

2. Batting average. Hits divided by number of times at bat.

3. Slugging average. Total bases (obtained from hits—not from errors, walks, or interference) divided by number of times at bat.

4. Fielding average. Total putouts and assists divided by total putouts, assists, and errors.

5. Earned run average for pitchers. Multiply earned runs allowed by nine; then divide by the number of innings pitched.

6. On-base percentage. Add up hits, walks, hit by pitches; divide it by the total of at bats, walks, hit by pitches, and sacrifice flies.

It would be absurd to award the batting title, for example, to someone who bats .500 by getting up twice and getting one hit, so there are minimum requirements for consideration in individual championships. To qualify for the batting or slugging championships, you have to have a number of plate appearances that exceeds 3.1 times the number of games in the season. Thus, in a normal 162-game season, you need 502 plate appearances to qualify. The only exception would be if there was someone with fewer than 502 plate appearances who would win anyway with his number of hits if he were credited with 502 plate appearances. Pitchers, to qualify for individual championships, have to have pitched as many innings as the number of games scheduled—in other words, a minimum of 162 innings in a normal season. To qualify for fielding records as a catcher, you have to catch in at least half the games played that season. Infielders and outfielders have to play their position in at least two-thirds of the games to be considered for individual field-ing championships at that position. Pitchers need to pitch that magic 162 innings if they want to be considered for the best-fielding pitcher in the league.

HOW TO TELL THE TRUTH WITH STATISTICS

These "official" percentages are dwarfed in number by the "unoffi-cial" statistics that can be derived from the official scorecards published for every game and that everyone in baseball uses. There are records for hits, doubles, triples, home runs, strikeouts, walks, hitting into double plays, stolen bases, caught stealing; there are batting averages figured for hitting with men in scoring position, no one on, and with various counts on the batter. Pitchers are tracked for the number of strikes and balls they throw, number of walks they give up, number of men they strike out, even the number of pitches they throw (and what kind of pitches they were). Fielders are graded on their *range factor*—add putouts and assists and divide by the number of games—which some consider a much more accurate indication of fielding ability than fielding average. Catchers get marks for throwing out base runners trying to steal.

With a little imagination, anyone can use the numbers gathered to dream up new ways of describing what goes on during a baseball game. Want to know how many strikeouts a pitcher averages in night games? How many double plays a batter hits into on artificial turf fields? How often a given hitter gets a hit off a lefty with men on base? How many times a pitcher throws over to first? A batter's average when he has two strikes on him? You can figure it out, and in fact someone undoubtedly already has. Over the past twenty years or so, baseball fan statisticians have begun to apply sophisticated techniques to analyzing the numbers, coming up with "new" statistics like "runs created," "pitching runs," and "stolen base wins." The Society for American Baseball Research and its publications are the source of many of these ideas. For those with a taste for mathematical formulas, check out *The Hidden Game of Baseball* by John Thorn and Pete Palmer.

THE BASEBALL RECORD THAT WILL NEVER BE BROKEN

This is a favorite argument among baseball fans, because everyone can make an assertion, and no one can be proven wrong—at least not today. Right now, in a bar somewhere in America, someone is asserting that Joe DiMaggio's 56-game hitting streak, Hank Aaron's 755 home runs, Cy Young's 512 wins are records that will never be broken. A record like Young's will never be broken because the nature of the game has changed so much that no pitcher will ever get the opportunity to win that many games. As for DiMaggio and Aaron, it's still perfectly conceivable that one of today's singles slappers will catch DiMaggio, or that a young slugger like Ken Griffey will equal Aaron. The problem, though, is that when you start to consider baseball records, things can get pretty silly. Most infield hits in a rain-delayed AstroTurf night game? Most foul balls during a single time at bat? Best lifetime ERA by a red-haired knuckleballer? Someone holds these records, and for all we know one of them will never be broken. But who cares? If you want to make sense of this discussion, first set the rules. The record has to be real—that is, it has to demonstrate a truly useful baseball skill. And it has to be realistic. There's no point, for example, in citing Johnny Vander Meer's record two no-hitters in a row—pitching three no-hitters in a row would be remarkable, but it depends on improbable coincidence as much as on skill. Single-game records, for purposes of this argument, aren't interesting for much the same reason. Good baseball isn't a burst of brilliant play in one game. It's the accumulation of a thousand little things done consistently over a long season, or over a long career. So let's narrow it down to season-long or lifetime accomplishments. Now here's a record that fills our criteria and truly resonates (and usually isn't mentioned in those discussions in bars): The best winning percentage among 300-game winners. Lefty Grove, who pitched for the Philadelphia Athletics and the Boston Red Sox in the 1920s and 1930s, won 300 games and had a winning percentage of .680. (Over one six-year period the guy went 152–41 for a .787 win percentage!) In second place is Christy Mathewson, who won 373 games with a winning percentage of .665. The only contemporary player who's anywhere near these two is Tom Seaver: 311 wins and only a .603 win percentage. Never's a long time, but just take it from me: Lefty Grove's record will never be broken.

Generally speaking, sabrmetricians view runs made by the offense and runs given up by the defense as the key to understanding the contributions of a baseball player to the success of his team. This makes perfect sense—the only way to win is to score more runs than the other team, so anything that helps you do this is good baseball. If you think stealing bases, for example, is helpful, you have to prove that stealing bases causes your team to score more runs than if you didn't steal. It's no good to say, as some do, "Well, the threat of stealing always upsets the pitcher, makes him pitch badly to the batter, so it naturally helps your team" unless you can prove that "upsetting the pitcher" causes more runs to score for your team. If it doesn't, then who cares whether the pitcher is upset or not? Thus, as Bill James explained in *The Baseball Abstract* in 1984, it doesn't really matter what a team's batting average is, because the team that has the best offense is the team that scores the most runs.

So a batter's job is not to hit home runs, or to hit for a high average, or to hit behind the runner, or to stay out of the double play, or any of the other things batters are supposed to do—all those are only means to an end. The batter's job is to create runs, period. And any legal way of doing it is just fine. So Bill James set out to try to create a formula that you could apply to a batter's accomplishments to figure out how many runs he created. This is what he came up with, and it works pretty well for the entire league and for individual teams—that is, you come very close to the number of runs actually scored if you apply this formula:

$$[(\text{Hits} + \text{Walks} - \text{Caught Stealing}) \times (\text{Total Bases} + .55 \text{ Stolen Bases})] \div (\text{At Bats} + \text{Walks}) = \text{Runs Created}$$

Because this works for the whole league and for whole teams, you can conclude that if you use it on an individual hitter, you'll find out how many runs he was actually responsible for during a season—and never mind how many RBIs he had or how high his batting average was. This gives some interesting results when the discussion of "the greatest season a hitter ever had" comes up. If you go purely by the number of runs created, the best season any hitter ever had was Babe Ruth's 1921 season. In 1927, when he hit 60 home runs, his runs created was actually lower than Lou Gehrig's. Yankee fans old enough to remember Mantle, but not Ruth and Gehrig, will say that Mickey Mantle's 1956 season was the greatest season ever by a hitter; but his 188 runs created in that year (his career best) puts him twenty-sixth on the all-time list. And, of course, great hitters have many great seasons: In the top twenty-five seasons in runs created, eight belong to Ruth, four to Gehrig, and three to Ted Williams.

The derivation of this formula (and lots of others) is all laid out in the old editions of *The Baseball Abstract*, so take a look if you're interested. Not everyone will want to read every word—James, by his own admission, can go on and on. *The Hidden Game of Baseball*, by John Thorn and Peter Palmer, is one of the most original works in baseball statistics. It is compact and lucid, and we recommend it highly. We've undoubtedly oversimplified things here, but we want to give you a taste of what sabrmetricians do and how much further their work can carry you in figuring out who's good and who isn't than the few traditional statistics baseball fans usually pay attention to.

Pitching and defense have been put under the same kind of statistical microscope in an attempt to figure out what the defense contributes in the way of preventing runs from scoring—which is the only legitimate aim of the defense. The same theory applies here: Fielding average, putouts, ERA, and so on don't tell you if the defense is working. The only thing that tells you how good a defense a team has is how good they are at preventing runs from scoring. So the sabrmetricians have come up with a way of figuring out how many runs a given player at a given position prevents from scoring. The formula is too involved to get into here, but essentially it considers several factors—putouts, assists, errors, and double plays, each weighted in different ways—to come up with a single number describing the contribution of the fielder. The formula varies depending on the position. For example, participation in double plays tells more about a second baseman's skill than it would about an outfielder's, so modifications are made to give each position its due.

The won-lost record of a pitcher depends at least as much on the team behind him as it does on the pitcher himself. Some pitchers get more run support than others from their teams, so they wind up with better won–lost averages. Statisticians, however, have worked out ways to account for these differences, thereby telling us much more about a pitcher's skill than a simple won–lost record alone. Some stadiums are *hitter's parks*—that is, batting averages in these parks are higher, more home runs are hit, and so on. So there are formulas that take into account the *park factor* to distinguish more accurately between, say, a hitter whose home field is Fenway Park, a notorious hitter's park, and one who plays in the Astrodome in Houston, a pitcher's park. (By the way, the park factor calculation is one of the most complex of the "new" statistics that sabrmetricians have developed. Essentially, it considers the number of runs scored by the visiting teams in each park and compares that to the average number of runs scored by visiting teams in all parks.)

ONE MORE REASON WE ALL HOPE TOMMY LASORDA LIVES FOREVER

"When I die, I want my tombstone to say, 'Dodger Stadium was his address, but every ballpark was his home.'"
—TOMMY LASORDA

With the proliferation of personal computers and software filled with data that can be manipulated at the touch of a few keys, anyone with a computer and a CD-ROM drive can now invent, and then collect, strange and wonderful statistics. Want a list of the top-ten winning left-handers in indoor stadiums? The best base stealers in extra-inning games? The pitchers with the most strikeouts in day games in 1972? It's all there, relatively easy to get at, and you can make of it what you will. Obviously, some of these statistics will prove more interesting than others—and people will continue to argue about their usefulness. There are even two kinds of managers, divided by their respect or distaste for statistics. One, which for lack of a better name we'll call the Lasorda type, likes to depend on his baseball instincts and experience, which he is convinced are more valuable than any list of numbers. The other, which we'll call the LaRussa type, reads reams of computer printouts before, after, and even during every game. The former type tends to chew tobacco, have a large potbelly, and spit copiously. The latter tends to have gone to law school. OK—we're kidding, of course. Tommy Lasorda is probably just as knowledgeable about stats as LaRussa (and we don't know whether Tommy chews tobacco or not). It's just that George Will, who interviewed the manager extensively for his book *Men at Work*, has convinced us that LaRussa is an intellectual giant, and even if this is just another one of Will's hilarious gags, we're willing to play along. Anyway, Tommy Lasorda and Tony LaRussa are both very successful managers, so you're not going to get in a fight with us about whether computers or instincts make for better baseball. But if you want to, it's quite easy to find someone with whom you can get into a fight about it.

OF TIME AND THE RIVER OF STATS

Does batting .325 in 1934 mean the same thing as batting .325 in 1994 or 1924 or 1904? Would Babe Ruth be able to hit today's split-finger fastball? Would Hank Aaron have hit 755 home runs if he had played before they changed the construction of baseballs to make them livelier? Questions like these have fueled baseball arguments for years, and the questions make considering records over time a difficult proposition. Home Run Baker got his nickname because he led the league in home runs four years in a row, 1911–1914. He had 11, 10, 12, and 9 homers in those years. Because you need about 45 home runs to lead the league today, does it make any sense to conclude that Baker wasn't much of a slugger? These questions are posed here not to elicit the answers, but only to illustrate how complex and multifaceted the study of baseball statistics can become.

STATISTICS YOU SHOULD KNOW, OR AT LEAST KNOW ABOUT

Enough books with lists of numbers are published to make any listings here superfluous. But it is useful and important for any baseball fan to understand the following:

I. Offense

Lifetime Games

You have to be good, or they don't keep writing your name on the lineup card every day. You have to be strong to keep up a high level of play day after day. And you have to stay healthy. Pete Rose tops this list and the list for most at bats as well.

Walks

Players who walk a lot are usually the most feared hitters. Often they're walked intentionally. More often, they're walked because pitchers are afraid of them and are "pitching around" them—that is, pitching around the edges of the plate because anything they put in the middle of the plate with these guys will likely turn into a hit. As with any lifetime record dependent on quantity rather than average, it helps to get up a lot—this is part of the reason Pete Rose is on the top-ten list for walks. Ted Williams, for example, accumulated 420 more walks than Rose and did it playing 1,270 fewer games.

Strikeouts

The list of batters who've struck out more than anyone else includes some of the greatest hitters of all time. Reggie Jackson was allowed to get up again and again despite all his strikeouts because he was very likely to hit a home run—in fact, he hit 563 of them, which makes up for a lot of strikeouts. Stargell, Schmidt, Bonds, Mantle—all are great hitters who made up for the strikeouts with impressive power. Ruth? 1,330 strikeouts, thirty-seventh on the All-Time Whiff List. Aaron is thirty-first with 1,383. On the other hand, Ted Williams was a slugger with good eyes: He had 521 homers, but only struck out 709 times. And if you want a home run hitter who really doesn't strike out a lot, look up DiMaggio, Joe: 361 homers, 369 strikeouts, a record that, like many things about DiMaggio, remains unmatched. Strikeouts are apparently more common today than they once were. Six of the top-ten worst single-season strikeout records occurred after 1986. Maybe today's managers are more willing to put up with the strikeouts if enough home runs are hit.

Batting Average

Among the top ten in lifetime batting average, only one man, Ted Williams, played later than 1937. Rule changes to alter the balance between pitcher and hitter have been a repeating theme in baseball history. In 1903, for example, the height of the pitcher's mound was fixed at "no more than fifteen inches" to prevent pitchers from using the laws of gravity to the batter's disadvantage, and in 1950 the fifteen-inch height was made mandatory. When all those home runs were hit in 1961, the year Maris broke Ruth's record, the major leagues decided that the strike zone was too small, giving batters too much of an advantage. So, in 1963, they officially made it bigger by a couple of inches. Then hitting started to decline—drastically. The nadir was reached in 1968, when the entire American League batted .230, and the batting crown was won by Carl Yastrzemski with a .301 average. With the balance going so much toward the pitcher, baseball responded in 1969 by changing the strike zone again, to make it smaller and lowering the pitcher's mound a full five inches.

Still, the overall trend in batting averages since the beginning of the century is clearly downward. Gloves are bigger than they once were. More games are played at night, which may be harder on batters than on pitchers. Some believe that the explanation is that pitchers are bigger and stronger and can throw harder, but the fast answer to this is that batters are bigger and stronger, too, so they should be holding their own. The harder travel schedules, the slider, and the split-finger fastball have also been suggested as factors in explaining the downward trend.

> *"You can't win all of the time. There are guys out there who are better than you."*
> —YOGI BERRA

What may be the most interesting and convincing theory to explain the disappearance of the .400 hitter belongs not to a baseball professional or a sportswriter but to a paleontologist: Stephen Jay Gould. As methods of playing baseball have become more refined over the years, Gould believes, extremes in batting averages (and we presume other statistics as well) will decline. That is, the best and worst individual averages in a given year will, over time, approach the average of all hitters. Now you can look this up— lowest averages each year—but it isn't easy. *The Baseball Encyclopedia* and many other sources list highest averages, but to find the lowest averages, you have to go through the complete records of all players each year looking for them. It is a measure of how compelling this sort of thing can be that Gould, who you would think would be busy with more important things—you know, tenured-professor-at-Harvard kind of things—actually took it upon himself to find the lowest averages in each year. And guess what! He's right! The difference between the average of all players and the average of the worst hitter has been getting smaller, and so has the difference between the average of all players and the average of the best hitter. You could say, in other words, that the worst hitters are better, and the best hitters worse, than they've ever been. (You could say this, but you wouldn't be quite right. It's probably more correct to say that everyone—worst hitters, best hitters, pitchers, and fielders—are all better than they've ever been.) Gould believes that with the increasing regularity of play, baseball has become a "science," thus removing the advantage once enjoyed by the extraordinary player. Thus, no more .400 hitters, but not too many more .210 hitters, either.

Hits

Pete Rose pursued the redoubtable Ty Cobb for this record and finally caught up with him, although he needed over 500 more games than Cobb to do so. Rose named his son after Cobb, which is only one indication of how obsessed Rose was with chasing him. Rose doesn't hold any single-season records, not even for hits, his specialty. Although he led the league seven times in hits, his single-season best, 230, puts him thirty-second on the all-time list. He ranks seventeenth in at bats, twenty-seventh in doubles. His best single-season runs total was 130, which doesn't even put him among the top 100 players. His best season for RBIs was 82, which puts him nowhere. He didn't walk much, either—106 walks in one season was his best, which gets him nowhere near the top 100. And for all his hustle, he only hustled himself to third base eleven times in his best season, which, while there's nothing wrong with it, doesn't get him into the top 100 in the triples department. Rose's record taken as a whole is a remarkable lifetime accomplishment, and there's no reason to run him down—he was a great player, a true All-Star, and I'd take him on my team any day. But his accomplishments should be viewed in proper perspective, which is easier to do now that we are no longer distracted by seeing his picture in the paper every morning flying headfirst into second base.

Doubles

The top-ten list for doubles includes a combination of power hitters and contact hitters. Pete Rose is second behind Tris Speaker on the all-time list. (We never said he couldn't hit.) If you want to infuriate a Red Sox fan, tell him that the only reason Yastrzemski is on this list is that it's ridiculously easy to hit doubles in Fenway Park and then express your astonishment that no other Boston Red Sox player is in the top ten. (Well, Speaker did play for Boston for a few years, but not in the current version of Fenway Park, and anyway he kept right on getting lots of doubles after he was traded to Cleveland.) Earl Webb, the man who hit more doubles in a single season than anyone else, did play in Fenway, and maybe someone in the mood for tormenting Red Sox fans (not much of a challenge, since they can be reduced to tears if you point out their successes, never mind their failures) will figure out how many of his doubles were hit there.

Doubles have declined somewhat since the heyday in the 1930s, but not as radically as triples or batting averages.

Triples

The top-ten list includes no one who played later than about 1920. Why has the number of triples declined steadily since the beginning of the century? Is it the same factor as the reason for the decline in batting averages? Before going to Stephen Jay Gould's interesting theory, let us also look at the increase in the size of gloves and the possible reluctance of modern managers to encourage runners to take that extra base. Remember the rule: Never make the first or last out at third. Maybe this tactic is used more today than it once was.

Home Runs

This record probably attracts more attention than any other. It has also given rise to some of the uglier incidents in baseball history.

When Roger Maris broke Babe Ruth's record for single-season home runs, Ford Frick, the commissioner of baseball, decided to put an asterisk in the record books to indicate that Maris had broken the record in a 162-game season, as opposed to Ruth's 154 games. No other record was treated this way, and Maris remained bitter about it until the day he died. What happened to Hank Aaron during the months and weeks leading up to his breaking Ruth's lifetime record of 714 homers—the anonymous obscene and racist letters, the death threats—exemplified some of the most depressing aspects of American life and the American character. If you read his autobiography, *I Had a Hammer*, you'll see that Aaron, a reflective man of immense dignity, has not recovered from that vile spectacle and probably never will.

Home run records were drastically affected by the introduction in 1920 of the "lively ball." Babe Ruth hit 29 homers in 1919, breaking the previous record of 27 set in 1884. In 1920, he hit 54; in 1921, 59. To be sure, he played in more games beginning in 1920 and essentially quit pitching, but it didn't hurt that starting that year the construction of the ball was changed. Supposedly, Australian yarn instead of American yarn was used, which made it springier, but probably more important was the fact that the yarn was wound much tighter, making the ball harder. The result was apparent everywhere in baseball: In 1919, 448 home runs were hit; in 1920, 630; and in

GRAND SLAM HOME RUNS

The best way to get runs in bunches is to load up the bases and then bang it out of the park. Lou Gehrig holds the lifetime record: 23 grand salamis. Willie McCovey is second with 18. Eddie Murray, who is still playing, has 17, tied with Ted Williams and Jimmie Foxx. Don Mattingly holds the record for grand slams in a season, with 6 in 1987.

1921, 937. Despite what people say whenever a bunch of home runs are hit (usually at the beginning of the season when things haven't had a chance to even out yet), the construction of the ball hasn't changed one bit since 1926 when the cushioned cork center was introduced, except that in 1975 cowhide covering was allowed in addition to the original horsehide.

The belief, expressed periodically, that the ball has been "juiced" to make it go farther is usually more passionately espoused by pitchers than by hitters.

Home run totals, unlike batting average and triples, have generally increased over the years. In 1930, 1,565 were hit; in 1940, 1,571; in 1950, 2,073; in 1960, 2,128. In 1970, there were half again as many teams, but together they hit more than half again as many homers: 3,429. The year 1980, with two extra teams, saw a decline in homers to 3,087. In 1990, the upward trend resumed: 3,317 home runs. Still, Ruth's record stood for thirty-four years before Maris broke it, and Maris has now held it even longer than Ruth did. (If you're over forty, this realization will depress you mightily.) More people are hitting more home runs, but no one is hitting more in one season than Maris. Nor is Hank Aaron's 755 lifetime home run record in any apparent jeopardy. Ken Griffey, Jr., hit 40 homers in 111 games in 1994, and no one will ever know what might have happened in that might-have-happened season. In any case, Junior has a lot of good years ahead of him.

Total Bases

Total bases equal total bases of all safe hits—walks, errors, advances by balks, or stolen bases, etc., do not count. If you hit 755 home runs, that's 3,020 total bases right there, so it isn't surprising to find Hank Aaron at the top of the list, followed by other home run hitters. Neither Cobb nor Rose hit many homers. But singles and doubles, of which they both hit plenty, can add up. Cobb is fourth on the list; Rose sixth.

Runs Batted In

Getting runs across the plate is the important thing, and RBI totals tell something—although, as we now know, not everything—about who does it best. All the single-season RBI records were set in the seventeen years following the introduction of the lively ball in 1920.

RBIs, most sabrmetricians agree, are very dependent on batting position, team ability, and the home park advantage. Obviously some players just have more opportunities to pick up RBIs. How many of Gehrig's RBIs, for example, are attributable to the fact that Ruth, who batted ahead of him, got on base so often? So don't count too much on a player's RBI totals for estimating his worth to a team.

Slugging Average

You remember the formula: total bases divided by number of times at bat. This gives you a good idea of who has power and who doesn't. There's another variation of this, developed by Branch Rickey in the 1950s, called Isolated Power. The formula is: Total Bases – Hits ÷ At Bats. This may give an even more accurate picture of pure power hitting by removing singles from the total bases calculation. Considering Isolated Power would put Ralph Kiner, Mike Schmidt, and Mickey Mantle in the lifetime top-ten list of power hitters; and Johnny Mize, Stan Musial, and Rogers Hornsby would move to twelfth, twenty-seventh, and forty-second, respectively. Six of the top-ten best season slugging averages are held by Babe Ruth. So is the eleventh.

On-Base Percentage

No one in the entire history of baseball has gotten on base more often than he has made out through an entire career. Only sixteen people have ever accomplished it in a single season (Babe Ruth did

STEALING HOME

Jackie Robinson did it 19 times in his career, which ties him with George Sisler and Frankie Frisch. Rod Carew did it 17 times, Lou Gehrig and Tris Speaker 15 times apiece. Babe Ruth did it 10 times. But the all-time champion stealer of home plate is Ty Cobb. He did it 54 times, 21 more times than Max Carey, the guy in second place.

it five times; Ted Williams did it three times, and Williams had two seasons when his on-base percentage was .499. No one else did it more than once.) If you want to know who the hardest person to get out is, lifetime on-base percentage is the place to look. The all-time pitcher's nightmare: Ted Williams.

Stolen Bases

Of the fifteen top single-season stolen base totals, all but two of them occurred earlier than 1891 or later than 1982. Until 1898, a hitter could be credited with a stolen base if he stretched a single into a double or a double into a triple, so this causes some inflation of nineteenth-century figures. But when batting averages and home runs increase, you can expect stolen bases to decline. Why try to steal bases when the next guy up is likely to get a hit anyway? But this doesn't entirely explain why stealing lots of bases seems to have been out of fashion until quite recently. Two of the top ten in stolen bases, Tim Raines and the self-confident Rickey Henderson, are still playing and still adding to their totals, though of course at a slower rate than when they were younger. Charles Comiskey participated in the stolen base orgy of 1887 and is the same Charles Comiskey who later owned the White Sox and for whom Comiskey Park in Chicago is named.

II. Defense

Wins

Nine of the top fifteen pitchers in wins also make the top-fifteen list for losses. Only good pitchers have long careers, but long careers eventually catch up with you. Cy Young is first on both lists. Of course, in building up lots of wins, it helps considerably to have a good team in back of you. There are many examples of pitchers who have done their jobs spectacularly, but wound up with poor won-lost records because their teams stank. Jim Bouton, in his famous book *Ball Four*, does quite a bit of complaining about this phenomenon. In 1985, for example, Fernando Valenzuela allowed no earned runs in his first four games—none!—but found himself with a 2–2 won-lost record thanks to the ineptitude of his teammates. The truly impressive pitchers are the ones who have good records despite playing for terrible teams.

One of the most remarkable seasons in this category was Steve Carlton's 1972 record with the Phillies. He went 27–10, for a .730 winning percentage, and also led the league with a 1.97 ERA. The Phillies that year won only 59 games all together and when Carlton wasn't involved in the decision, their winning percentage was .269.

Almost all of the top 100 or so best in the single-season wins department occurred before the turn of the century. Pitchers used to start many more games than they start today. In 1892, for example, Cy Young started 49 games, and an average year for him included about 40 starts. And pitchers could also take it easy: Allowing a hit or so an inning was no big deal. No pitcher today could do that and still have a career in the majors. Pitchers today throw hard; their arms tire quickly. Relief pitchers and closers—pitchers who specialize in pitching the last inning or two of a game—are always warmed up and ready, and it's a pretty sure thing that with baseball as it is now, no one is going to come very close to Cy Young, in either wins or losses.

Earned Run Average

ERA, the number that indicates how many runs a pitcher allows per nine innings, tells you something more about a pitcher than his won–lost record. It takes out of consideration unearned runs—that is, the runs presumably due not to the pitcher's failures but to his teammates' errors and misplays. It also makes the records of relief pitchers more accurate—their won-lost record tells you even less than that of a starter, because they often don't get credit for either a win or a loss. An ERA of under 3.0 makes you a very good pitcher indeed. Under 2.0 for a season—only two pitchers, both of whom played in the late nineteenth century, have ever done it for an entire career—makes you exceptional.

ERA was established as an official statistic in 1912 in the National League and in 1913 in the American League. For some years after that, runs attributable to stolen bases were not counted as earned. Today they are, which makes sense because the pitcher is certainly as responsible as anyone else for runners who steal bases. ERA, like any stat, has its limitations. Good fielders can lower a pitcher's ERA; a hitter's park can make it soar. Even the relief staff can affect it: If a manager leaves a pitcher in too long because he doesn't have good relievers, that pitcher is liable to allow runs to score that otherwise wouldn't have. Sabrmetricians have tried to address some of these problems by adjusting ERA for league average and home park factor.

Opponents' Batting Average

This presents, perhaps, a purer picture of a pitcher's performance than ERA. It's simply the combined batting average of all the batters a given pitcher has faced. It is at least as clear a measure of success for a pitcher as batting average is for a hitter, because it's simply its mirror image. If a pitcher can keep this number under .210 or so for a single season, or about .240 for a career, he's among the best. Jerry Koosman, pitching for the Mets in 1977, went 8–20 with a team that came in dead last in its division. But his opponents only managed a .232 batting average against him, so it's fair to conclude that he was doing his best while his teammates were doing their worst.

The year of the pitcher was 1968. That's the year that a .301 batting average was enough to win the American League batting crown. Still, Luis Tiant put in one hell of a season with the Red Sox that year, allowing opponents a wretched .168 average.

Walks and Strikeouts

Nolan Ryan and Steve Carlton rank number one and number two in lifetime strikeouts. They also rank one and two in lifetime walks. Bob Feller and Phil Niekro also rank very high in both walks and strikeouts. Feller, in fact, led the league in both walks and strikeouts four times in his career. This may seem paradoxical, but it's not. These are the power pitchers. They throw hard, and when they're on, they're impossible to hit. But when they're not, no one knows where the ball might wind up. Wildness itself can work in their favor—it makes a hitter start to think. And as Yogi says, you can't hit and think at the same time. In the 1950s, the Yankees had a reliever, Ryne Duren, who wore thick glasses and threw ninety-five-mile-per-hour fastballs. He'd come into a game, squint toward the catcher, and throw his first warm-up pitch into the screen 60 feet behind the home plate. Now that gives a hitter something to think about.

The control pitchers, on the other hand, don't walk a lot of people, but they don't strike out many, either. The list of pitchers with the fewest walks per game has almost no overlap at all with the list of pitchers with the most strikeouts per game. Even the control pitchers with the most strikeouts don't set any records: In 1904, Cy Young struck out 200 and walked only 29, but he didn't lead the league in strikeouts—Rube Waddell had a remarkable 349 that year. The only man ever to strike out more than 3,000 and walk fewer than 1,000 in a career is Ferguson Jenkins. In general, if you want a lot of strikeouts, you're going to have to put up with a lot of walks.

Pitching rules changed frequently and radically before 1900. Until 1884, for example, pitchers weren't allowed to throw overhand—underhand and sidearm only were allowed. The results of that change were thousands of strikeouts in 1884. The changes weren't always in favor of pitchers. In fact, after pitchers seemed to be gaining the upper hand, the rules were changed in 1887 so that four strikes were allowed (and five balls), and walks were counted as hits. But this resulted in such outlandishly high batting averages that the changes were reversed, and pitching dominated again.

Then in 1893, the distance from batter to pitcher was set, effectively, at 60 feet 6 inches—5 feet farther back than it had been. This, of course, helped hitters considerably—in 1894, the National League ERA was 5.32, and the league batting average .309. The introduction of the lively ball in 1920 ushered in another hitter's era. Batting averages went up, home runs became common, and strikeouts declined.

There were more strikeouts before 1900, but the best strike-out-per-game numbers ("per game" as used here means "per nine innings") have been recorded in recent years. The best pitchers don't pitch as often as they used to, but when they do, they seem to be more effective, at least when measured by their rate of strikeouts. The best power pitchers today strike out between three and four more batters per game than the best before the turn of the century, despite the higher strikeout totals in those early years. Closers like Dennis Eckersley, who only pitches one or two innings in a game, can throw with all their might without fear of tiring. This, too, probably leads to more strikeouts per game.

Saves

Since 1969, relief pitchers have been credited with saves. (See Chapter 2 for the definition of a save.) Until then, no one bothered to record them, at least not officially, although of course they now have been researched and recorded for years prior to 1969. Saves have become much more common, and all the records for saves are held by pitchers in recent years.

Whereas it used to be that relievers were the worst pitchers on the staff, second stringers brought in only in emergencies, now relief pitching is a specialty essential to every team. And some closers—pitchers brought in to finish the last one or two innings of a game—are among the highest paid superstars of the game. This revolution in pitching strategy has made records of complete games irrelevant—completing a game is no longer a measure of a pitcher's worth. And it has made individual wins somewhat less important, too. Relievers come in too often to allow for many 20-game winners any more. Even ERA is a less-revealing stat than it used to be. A pitcher who leaves two men on base can be saved by a reliever who throws a double play ball to the first batter and ruined by one who lets those two men score.

To replace some of these numbers, there is now a statistic called a *quality start*. A quality start is credited to a starting pitcher if he pitches at least six innings and allows no more than three earned runs. The reasoning here is that that should be enough to keep his team in the game and allow the relievers to do their job. Even though this is not yet an official statistic approved by the Rules Committee (see page 186), it's becoming more and more commonly used. Now when you hear a TV announcer use the term, and they often do, you'll know what he's talking about.

OK, SO WHO'S REALLY THE BEST BASEBALL PLAYER EVER?

There is a real answer to this question—based not on who your favorite player is, or which team you root for, or which player was nice enough to give your kid an autograph last time you were at the park. To figure out who the best player is, you have to figure out who contributed the most runs to his team. And to figure out who the best pitcher is, you have to figure out who prevented the most runs from scoring against his team.

In Chapter 3, we listed the five qualities that scouts look for in judging baseball talent: hitting for average, hitting for power, fielding, running, and throwing. The best player, as all agree, is the player who does all these things best. And all of these talents can be summed up in a single number, called Overall Player Runs, a number that expresses how many runs a given player is responsible for by his efforts in each of these categories. John Thorn and Pete Palmer worked out the formula, which they published in *The Hidden Game of Baseball*. Here it is:

Overall Player Runs = Batting Runs + Base-Stealing Runs + Defensive Runs – Average Defensive Skill at the Position

The terms to the right of the equal sign here may not be familiar, and a detailed understanding of all of them requires more space than we have here (or in our head, come to think of it). But here are some brief definitions. The essential point to keep in mind is that runs are the important thing; scoring runs and preventing the other team from scoring them is what wins ball games and makes a player worth his salary.

Batting Runs: The derivation is quite complex, depending on batting order, year of play, and other factors, but the number expresses how many runs a player contributes above or below the league average (defined as zero) with his bat.

Base-Stealing Runs: Multiply the number of steals by .3 and the number of caught stealings by –.6. Add the two products, and that tells you how many runs you produce—or lose—by stealing. (You have to succeed overwhelmingly at base stealing to do your team more good than harm.)

Defensive Runs: A formula, modified slightly for different positions, that includes putouts, double plays, assists, and errors, and produces a number approximating the number of runs a fielder prevents with his glove.

Average Defensive Skill at the Position: This number, arrived at using a somewhat involved formula, gives credit to players who play the more difficult positions—middle infielders and the catcher—and puts their comparison on a par with, say, left fielders, who, however good they may be, don't contribute as much defensively because of where they're playing.

Finally, you take the result, overall player runs, and convert it to overall player wins—how many wins the player is himself responsible for. The number of runs required to produce one extra win varies over the years between nine and eleven (this can be calculated each year using the number of runs actually scored by a team). So for every ten or so overall player runs a player produces, he's adding one win to his team's record.

You'll have to trust us on this—that's a nonstatistician's non-mathematical summary of how you can decide who's really the best player. Thorn and Palmer have worked out parallel ways of figuring out who is the best pitcher, but we'll leave you to read about the derivations in *The Hidden Game of Baseball*. We use the same form as Thorn and Palmer.

So here it is: the end of all arguments and discussions of who's the best. First, the best pitchers ever.

LIFETIME PITCHER WINS SINCE 1901

1. Walter Johnson	73.3
2. Cy Young	69.7
3. Pete ("Grover") Alexander	60.5

(CONTINUED ON NEXT PAGE)

LIFETIME PITCHER WINS SINCE 1901 (CONTINUED)

4. Christy Mathewson	51.6
5. Lefty Grove	50.9
6. Tom Seaver	45.0
7. Bob Gibson	44.8
8. Warren Spahn	41.9
9. Ed Walsh	37.3
10. Gaylord Perry	37.1
Steve Carlton	37.1

LIFETIME PITCHER WINS SINCE 1961

1. Tom Seaver	45.0
2. Bob Gibson	44.8
3. Gaylord Perry	37.1
Steve Carlton	37.1
5. Phil Niekro	36.7
6. Jim Palmer	35.4
7. Don Drysdale	33.3
8. Bert Blyleven	28.8
9. Ferguson Jenkins	28.7
10. Juan Marichal	27.4

And finally, here they are: the best players ever—no need to discuss it further. These are the guys who with their hitting, defense, baserunning, stealing, throwing—everything except their good looks—won more games for their teams than anyone else in the history of the universe.

LIFETIME PLAYER WINS SINCE 1901

1. Babe Ruth	116.9
2. Ted Williams	96.9
3. Hank Aaron	89.9
4. Ty Cobb	89.3
5. Willie Mays	87.7
6. Nap Lajoie	85.3
7. Rogers Hornsby	82.6
8. Tris Speaker	81.0
9. Eddie Collins	80.0
10. Honus Wagner	79.3

LIFETIME PLAYER WINS SINCE 1961

1. Hank Aaron	89.9
2. Willie Mays	87.7
3. Frank Robinson	70.7
4. Joe Morgan	67.7
5. Mike Schmidt	64.8

(CONTINUED ON NEXT PAGE)

Lifetime Player Wins Since 1961 (continued)

6. Carl Yastrzemski	47.1
7. Al Kaline	46.8
8. Reggie Jackson	43.3
9. Rod Carew	42.8
10. Bobby Grich	42.3

Boy, we're glad we finally got that settled! What? You mean you still want to argue?

5

They Also Serve: Owners, Managers, Coaches, and Umpires

Many people besides ballplayers are required to make Major League Baseball work. Managers and umpires are on the field at every game, and you'll want to know what they're up to and why they act the way they do. Knowing about owners is probably less important to the pleasure of watching a game—some might say it detracts from it—but they are in the newspapers often enough that most fans are a little curious about them and at least casually interested in their exploits. In times of labor strife—which, in baseball, means most of the time—they become even more interesting, sometimes quite appalling. Coaches do more than just stand there and shout encouragement, and it's worth knowing what their contribution is. And umpires are people, too.

All fans know that baseball on the major league level is at least partly show business. Show business demands large personalities and elaborate gestures, and baseball has plenty of them. So let's look at the personalities and functions of some of these peripheral actors (and the occasional actress) who may sometimes distract us from what should be the center of our attention.

WANNA BUY A BASEBALL TEAM?

The very rich, as we are repeatedly reminded, are not like you and me. But they're not much like each other, either. Some very rich people subsidize art museums, some underwrite ballet companies, some give money for named chairs at universities or medical schools, and some buy baseball teams. When the National League added two new teams in 1993, the Colorado Rockies and the Florida Marlins, the people who bought the franchises paid $95 million for each of them. Teams didn't always cost that much, but they have always been expensive. A baseball team is not a business you can start in your garage. You have to be very rich to begin with. So almost all baseball owners make most of their money from something else, whether it's banking, beef, boats, or Buicks.

Let's take banking first. In 1969, each league expanded from ten to twelve teams, and the price of entry was $10 million. That's what C. Arnholt Smith paid to establish a franchise in San Diego. Smith was the owner of the United States National Bank, an institution with which Smith temporarily held the record for the country's largest bank failure. Smith's competence as a banker was amply matched by his competence as a baseball owner. According to Buzzie Bavasi, a forty-five-year veteran of the baseball business with the Dodgers, Angels, and Padres, Smith "never understood baseball or anything necessary to run a club." He quickly turned the Padres into a losing proposition and then decided it was time to sell. He accepted an offer of $12.5 million from Joe Danzansky, a grocery store chain operator with ideas about moving the Padres to Washington, D.C., who failed to realize that Smith had to have the permission of the league to accept any offer and that he had to get out of the lease he'd signed for the stadium with the city of San Diego. No sale.

Smith had a great deal of money, to be sure, but it turned out that not all the money he had belonged to him. In fact, Smith's total ignorance of the baseball business was the least of his problems. One day an IRS agent came to Bavasi's office and told him that the government was owed $26,753,420.42 in taxes Smith had neglected to pay. Bavasi reached in his pocket and offered to "make it even" by giving him forty-two cents. The agent, unaccountably, didn't find this funny.

In the meantime, things were going from bad to worse with the baseball team. The Padres were awful on the field; attendance was terrible; and the whole enterprise was so strapped for cash that they'd reached a point where (according to Bavasi) they would give players their checks on Friday and ask them not to try to cash them until the next week. Once an umpire picked up a base to give it as a souvenir to Lou Brock, who had broken a stolen base record, and all Bavasi could do was sit in the stands, fuming—a $52 base, down the drain! Such was the desperation to which Padres management had been driven.

When Smith's tax problems came to court, he was quickly found guilty as charged of tax evasion, and the Feds wound up taking their share out of the money Smith got when he finally succeeded in selling the team. Bavasi, who owned 32 percent of the club, found out that the IRS would be getting his share, too, and there wasn't much he could do about it. Eventually Smith would have to pay $30 million in civil fraud damages to investors in his U.S. National Bank. Bavasi is a man who will no doubt understand when we say that baseball owners can be colorful.

Enough about banking. On to beef. Ray Kroc, whose qualifications for running a baseball team were having $12 million and considerable experience with hamburgers, was the man bold enough to buy the pathetic San Diego team in 1974. The Padres opened the season that year by dropping three games on the road before making their home debut, which for some reason almost forty thousand fans had come to see. Late in the game, the Padres were losing by seven runs when Kroc decided to take matters into his own hands. He marched into the announcer's booth, grabbed the microphone, and intoned to those fans masochistic enough to have stayed until the eighth inning, "I've got some good news and some bad news. The good news is that you loyal fans of San Diego have outstripped Los Angeles. They had thirty-one thousand on opening night. We have almost forty thousand tonight, our home opener. And the bad news is that I've never seen such stupid ballplaying in my life." Jaws dropped all over Major League Baseball. The commissioner demanded an apology, which Kroc proffered, and the National League president made the announcer's booth officially off limits to everyone but the announcers. But Marvin Miller, head of the Players Association, had the last word on this incident: "The players of the San Diego and Houston clubs have demonstrated by their restraint in the face of Mr. Kroc's inexcusable insults that their intelligence far exceeds his." No one, so far as we know, has ever convincingly refuted Miller's assertion.

After Kroc died, his widow, apparently not as much of a baseball fan as her late husband, wanted to give the Padres to the city of San Diego. Her fellow owners roundly rejected the idea in 1990. Baseball owners don't mind if a city wants to subsidize them at public expense—twenty-three of twenty-eight teams, all of whose owners are, no doubt, firm believers in free enterprise and opposed to government interference in business, receive immense amounts of taxpayer money to help pay for their stadiums. But the last thing they want is for a baseball team's business to be exposed to public scrutiny.

Andrew Zimbalist, in his book *Baseball and Billions,* points out that it's very difficult to get information about owners. Most of them keep themselves far away from fans, researchers, or sportswriters, and with good reason. Whenever one of them does get in the papers, it is almost always in connection with some scandal or peculiar behavior. George Steinbrenner, the boat builder and convicted felon who is principal owner of the New York Yankees, is a case in point. He, along with some partners, bought the Yankees from CBS for about $10 million in 1973. He promised he'd be an absentee owner and stick to building boats. The next year, his absenteeism was made official: He was suspended from baseball for fifteen months for having made illegal campaign contributions to Richard Nixon in 1972. Although Steinbrenner certainly isn't the only baseball owner to fire managers on a regular basis, he has probably fired more of them, and with much more flair, than any of his colleagues. His firing of Yogi Berra in the early weeks of the 1985 season must have been particularly egregious. Berra has refused to set foot in Yankee Stadium again while Steinbrenner is running the team and has been conspicuous in his absence even for tributes to his old teammates, which Steinbrenner schedules on a regular basis. (Steinbrenner's attitude toward his employees and ex-employees is not a model of consistency. He hired Billy Martin four times as manager, fired him four times, and then staged a "Billy Martin Day" at Yankee Stadium at which he retired Martin's number. The Yankees have a lot of retired numbers, but none of the others belongs to a .257 lifetime hitter.)

> *"When I was a kid, I wanted to join the circus and play baseball. With the Yankees, I got to do both."*
> —GRAIG NETTLES

In any case, maybe Steinbrenner should have been suspended from the shipbuilding business, too—for his own protection. He must have made some money at one time in that business, but he managed to rack up $21.8 million in losses between 1986 and 1990. In this case, Steinbrenner was unable to fire the manager, because his manager was himself. Nonetheless, he's done pretty well for himself in baseball. When the team signed a twelve-year cable contract with Madison Square Garden Network, they got $500 million for it, and Steinbrenner and his partners pocketed $100 million for themselves.

Even his fellow owners don't trust him. Jerry Reinsdorf, owner of the Chicago White Sox, called him a habitual liar and did it out loud in public. "How do you know when George Steinbrenner is lying?" he asked and then answered his own question: "When his lips are

George Steinbrenner, owner of the New York Yankees, after the 1978 World Series. It's hard to tell whether first baseman Jim Spencer is celebrating the victory or taking advantage of an opportunity to assault his boss. In any case, this is one of Steinbrenner's more dignified moments. *National Baseball Library & Archive, Cooperstown, NY*

moving." Fay Vincent, the former baseball commissioner, who made Steinbrenner relinquish operational control of the Yankees in 1990 because of his involvement with a gambler and convicted extortionist named Howard Spira, was equally unrestrained in his characterization of the Yankee owner, whose activities he described as "a pattern of behavior that borders on the bizarre."

You want bizarre? Although her friend Steinbrenner gets all the press because he's in New York, out in Cincinnati, Marge Schott, the principal owner of the Cincinnati Reds, really knows how to put on a show. She's not too familiar with baseball, however. After Pete Rose was banned from baseball for betting on games, Steinbrenner suggested she replace him as manager with Lou Piniella. "Lou who?" asked Marge.

Schott, who is often photographed with her St. Bernard dogs, took over the Reds in 1985. She is the owner of a car dealership in Cincinnati, and she doesn't let any other car dealers advertise in the Reds' scorecard or yearbook. She herself, however, does advertise her Buicks and Chevrolets in those places, as well as on the stadium fences and on the Reds' radio broadcasts, and she charges herself considerably reduced rates. Or at least that's what her partners claimed in a suit they filed against her in 1989. She doesn't like it if her players get involved with other car dealers, either. Star outfielder Eric Davis once signed on to promote BMWs, which made Marge angry, so she told him it wasn't allowed. When Davis' agent gently explained to her that she didn't have the power to tell players what to endorse or not endorse, she decided to use persuasion: She gave Davis a Corvette to help convince him not to get involved with BMWs. Then she turned around and charged the cost of the Corvette to the baseball team.

Her partners think she's been robbing them blind. They claimed that between 1986 and 1988 she hid more than $5 million in income from them, made them pay for a scoreboard twice, and showed partnership receipts of $2.06 million while at the same time distributing $3.75 million to herself. The partners also claimed that she double-charged them for computers, repairs to the AstroTurf on the field, improvements at the spring training facility, and many other unspecified expenditures. The suit was settled in 1991, but the terms of the settlement are a secret. Her partners might accuse her of stealing money, but they certainly couldn't accuse her of wasting it. She once took the leftover doughnuts from a company meeting and tried to sell them to her office employees. Her partners didn't demand a share of the doughnut income in their suit against her, nor is it known what income she reported to the IRS from this enterprise.

One of Schott's problems is that she can't resist performing in public. Before the first game of the 1990 World Series, she decided she had to give a speech to the assembled multitudes—and to the millions of people sitting in front of their TV sets at home. The commissioner didn't want her to go out on the field, but just before the National Anthem was to be played, she strolled up to the microphone. "We're dedicating this World Series to our wonderful women and men over in the Far East that are serving us," she said, apparently forgetting that World War II was over and that the troops at the time were in Kuwait.

Somewhat less amusing than her financial shenanigans and her performances on the field is her attitude toward races and religions that are not her own. According to Jerry Crasnick, writing in *Baseball America*, Tim Sabo, the Reds' controller, claimed that Schott specifically instructed him not to hire any blacks for front office work because "I don't want their kind here." She doesn't care much for Jews, either. Her vulgar tirades are well known and too depressing to reproduce here. Some found Schott's ignorance and buffoonery tolerable for a while, but as more and more of her repellent bigotry became public, and as Schott's unapologetic attitude became more widely known, even the owners' Executive Council had had enough. Eventually, after the intervention of Jesse Jackson and several high-priced lawyers, they suspended her from baseball for one year, made her attend "multicultural training programs," and fined her $25,000 (the maximum allowed under the Major League Agreement). The suspension meant little. Schott still was a general partner in the team and would continue to be so. She was still allowed to attend games, although she wasn't allowed on the field or in her regular seat near the dugout. She kept Jim Bowden, her own man, as general manager, and she was permitted to handle big business items like TV contracts, concessions, advertising, and banking decisions. She has been trying to temper her language, at least in public.

Are all baseball owners ill-mannered, uninformed, unprincipled, greedy, shameless, and hopelessly deficient in moral sense or ordinary human decency? Of course not. Maybe we have that impression because of the ones whose names most often appear in the newspapers. Yet there are exceptions: Peter Angelos, owner of the Baltimore Orioles, is one of them. While his fellow owners were planning to replace major league players with "replacement players" during the strike of 1994–95, he was the only owner who opined that Major League Baseball players were, in fact, not actually replaceable by anyone except other major league players—and all the major league players he knew about were out on strike. So he announced that he wasn't going to put the Baltimore Orioles on the field until the strike was settled. His fellow owners were, of course, baffled by this enunciation of principle and threatened to impose fines if he followed through on his threat. Fortunately for everyone, the strike ended before Angelos had to act. Nelson Doubleday, co-owner of the New York Mets, quietly runs an efficient organization, hires intelligent baseball people whom he trusts to work for him, and then butts out, setting an example that too few other owners are willing to follow. Owners like these are, alas, the exceptions.

WHAT A MANAGER DOES

"One of the things about baseball I've always liked is that it's transparent. There are no secret moves, no trick plays, no offensive set used for the first time in the season. Major league managers never trick other major league managers."

—KEITH HERNANDEZ

The range of possibilities under baseball's rules is narrowly limited. Keith Hernandez is mostly right; there may be a few trick plays in baseball, but everyone already knows about them, and they are rarely used at the major league level. Every major league manager pretty much knows what possibilities are open to any manager on the opposing team. So you can't show a brand-new defense or a play that's never been tried before. But a manager must apply the infinite range of his team's talents to the set number of non-trick plays that baseball rules allow. Here is where the manager's talents are most important: in deciding what skills he has on his team and how best to exploit them in any given situation. There's no point in settling on a tactic of, say, bunting and stealing bases if all you have is a team full of slow-footed sluggers. Don't trade for a home run hitter if you play half your games in the Astrodome—look for speed, because that's how games are won there. Do all your pitchers do best on four days' rest, the standard amount? Or are there some who need more work and would be better off pitching every other day? Do you have a right-handed hitter on your team who, contrary to expectation, does better against righties? Then maybe he should be platooned in exactly the opposite way you would expect to platoon a hitter.

Whitey Herzog, longtime manager of the St. Louis Cardinals, was a master of this kind of manipulation of players' skills and tendencies. Herzog, unlike most managers, didn't get fired a lot during his eighteen-year career, which ended in 1990 (he's still in baseball, though no longer as a field manager). He managed only four teams all together (if you count the six games he managed for the Angels in 1974), and he spent his last eleven years managing the Cardinals. Herzog, like most managers, kept careful track of what his players could do. He has written notes on every opposing hitter he has ever faced and on every ball those players have ever hit against his pitchers. He has records on every pitch his pitchers have ever thrown and where the opposing batter hit the ball. With notes on every hitter, every pitcher, and every move any of them has made against any of the others, he has the database of information required to make intelligent decisions. Herzog, like most good managers, plays the percentages and knows that what hitters and pitchers have done in the past is an extremely good predictor of what they'll do in the future.

Whitey Herzog liked Gussie Busch, who owned the Cardinals, and he got on well with Gene Autry of the Angels; but for most owners, he had what might generously be described as contempt. In his autobiography, *White Rat: A Life in Baseball*, he got his licks in:

CHARLES FINLEY, OAKLAND A'S:

"Finley was a real crackpot."

M. DONALD GRANT, N.Y. METS:

"He was a stockbroker, a guy who didn't know beans about baseball but thought he did. I've run into a lot of guys like Donald Grant in my career, and everywhere they show up, they're trouble."

BOB SHORT, TEXAS RANGERS:

"Bob Short was a fast-buck artist, a man who would do anything for a buck, a man who never had a long-term plan in his life. He had no earthly idea how to run a baseball team."

EWING KAUFFMAN, KANSAS CITY ROYALS:

"I never really got along with Ewing Kauffman, the owner of the club, and his wife, Muriel, hated my guts. People would tell me they'd overhear the Kauffmans . . . saying I was getting too much credit for the club's success and how they should get rid of the son of a bitch. I was never sure of what I'd done wrong."

Sometimes, the received wisdom doesn't work. Righties, as we know, are supposed to hit left-handed pitchers better than right-handed pitchers. Jack Clark, however, was an exception. He was a righty, but right-handed pitching never bothered him. Then Herzog noticed that there was an exception to the exception: For some unknown reason, Clark couldn't hit righty Rick Reuschel. Only detailed notes would have revealed this fact, but of course Herzog had the notes. So every time Reuschel played, Herzog benched Clark.

Managers of most teams have a good deal to say about trades and other player personnel moves. Usually the general manager, or in some cases the owner, of the team has the last word on trades, but the field manager almost always plays an important role. When Herzog managed the Cardinals, he was very much in charge of such matters, although of course salaries were decided by the owner.

Managers of major league teams have almost all played ball themselves, but for some reason very few of them were much good. Whitey Herzog was an outfielder for Washington, Kansas City, and Baltimore, but he spent most games sitting on the bench and finished his eight-year career with a .257 batting average. Tony LaRussa is considered one of the most intelligent managers in the big leagues, but his six-year playing career, in which he got into maybe twenty games a year, ended with a .199 batting average. Bobby Cox, another longtime and very successful manager, had a two-year career in the majors as a player, during which he accomplished very little. There are some exceptions: Lou Piniella was a star player; Frank Robinson was twice an MVP; Mike Hargrove was a standout for Texas and Cleveland. But a more typical picture is presented by Buck Showalter, Kevin Kennedy, and Jim Leyland—managers who never played a single game in the big leagues. Talent as a player and talent as a manager are, clearly, two separate things.

Of the twenty-eight managers in the majors who started the 1995 season, eight were once catchers. Considering how many more

FORMER CATCHERS AS MANAGERS: TWO VIEWS

"They probably study the whole game. They're more studious about the game."

—DOUG MELVIN, GENERAL MANAGER, TEXAS RANGERS

"I've known a lot of dumb catchers. Just because you're a catcher doesn't mean you're going to make a good manager."

—BOB BOONE, FORMER CATCHER AND CURRENT MANAGER, KANSAS CITY ROYALS

players are at the other positions, this is a very high number. It may be that catching is good preparation for managing. The catcher is in on every conversation at the mound. It's the catcher to whom the manager talks most about the pitching staff, and it's the catcher who is, in a sense, managing the pitching staff in every game. Unlike any other player, he faces his teammates and can see where all of them are playing. He makes most of the decisions on what pitches will be thrown. He's thinking about strategy on every pitch, just like a manager. Jim Leyland feels that catchers are more concentrated, more involved in the game's strategy than any other player, which gives them a good feeling for the way a manager must think.

A manager's day begins early and ends late. Twelve-hour days are not unusual during the season, so even when they're playing at home, which is only half the time, major league managers probably don't see too much of their families. Most managers begin their day some eight hours before game time with a meeting with their coaches to go over the opposing team's players. This is not a casual discussion, but a detailed report, backed by hard data, on what each player on the other team has done, can do, and is likely to do in tonight's game. Players usually show up about three hours before the game, and the manager will meet with them and his coaches to go over the team they're facing that night. Again, the discussions are detailed, concentrating on the little things that can mean the difference between success and failure: Try running on this pitcher—he balks a lot; this batter has trouble with a fastball on the outside part of the plate; the leadoff hitter bunted for a base hit in two games in the past three weeks; we watched that guy in batting practice, and he's trying to pull the ball.

Of course, it's the players who play and win (or lose), not the managers. But talented players have to demonstrate their talents at the right moment, in the right situation. Making sure that they do so is the manager's job. This means taking advantage of a player's special skills—even good players are not equally good at everything. For example, picture this: It's late in the game, score tied, one out, and a man on first. Everybody and his grandmother (provided she read Chapter 3 of this book) is getting ready for a hit-and-run. But the manager has to think first: Is this pitcher wild? Is my batter a good contact hitter? Is my runner fast? No matter how perfect the situation is for a hit-and-run, unless the answers to these questions come up right—that is, no, yes, and yes—then maybe a hit-and-run isn't such a hot idea. It's the manager's job to know the answers to these questions, process them quickly, and arrive at a decision. A lot of detailed information about each player—his own and the other team's—goes into answering even the simplest questions of baseball strategy, and the manager has to be on top of it all.

COACHES

In most Little League and high school games, one of the players—usually one who's a bench sitter anyway—gets coaxed into coaching first or third base. The usual contribution at this level is shouts of encouragement, with the occasional admonition to "Get back!" or "Go for second!" At the major league level, the theory may be pretty much the same, but the practice is a bit more formalized.

"Keep your eye on the ball" isn't always good advice in Major League Baseball. A hitter, for example, facing a ninety-five-mile-per-hour fastball, probably isn't physiologically capable of "keeping his eye on the ball." And in running to first base, although it is certainly possible to keep your eye on the ball, it isn't necessarily desirable. Most first base coaches will want their runner to look at first base—or at the coach himself—rather than following the ball with his eyes, which will slow down his progress. After the runner rounds first, it's a different story—then he has to know where the ball is. The first base coach will help him find it, and then advise him on whether he should head for second or hold up at first. You usually can't hear him, but the first base coach often shouts at the runner. "Make your turn!" means go around the base and start to head for second. "No, no!" is a directive to hold up at first. "Go for two!" means exactly what it says. You'll also see him pointing toward second, usually with both hands, to indicate where he wants the runner to go.

Once a runner reaches first, the first base coach will remind him of certain fundamentals. "Find the ball" is a frequent phrase—in other words, see the ball in the pitcher's hand before you take a lead off the base. Two or three times a season, a major leaguer gets tagged out when he takes a lead without noticing that the pitcher doesn't have the ball: the ancient hidden ball trick. Many major leaguers—and especially those caught by it—consider the hidden ball trick bush league; but as long as runners fall for it, fielders will keep using it. The first base coach will also remind the runner how many are out and point out whether some of the outfielders are playing deep enough for him to take an extra base when the time comes. He may also tell the runner to adjust his lead or remind him of the catcher's throwing ability or that of the outfielders. "Make sure he pitches" is a typical first base coach's admonition not to run too soon. All this seems elementary, and it is, but even in the Show a few reminders can be useful, and sensible players are not insulted.

After the runner passes first base, he's in the hands of the third base coach. The third base coach will have as many reminders of the obvious as the first base coach. He also has to help the runner decide whether to go to third base and, having gone to third, whether to go home. The third base coach will watch the shortstop and second baseman to warn a runner on second of pickoff moves, and he'll keep an eye on the third baseman to prevent pickoffs at third. Obviously, the runners themselves have to be watching out for this, but the coach is there to remind them in case attention flags. The coach also advises the runner on third about tagging up—when he should stand on the base with a long fly, or go halfway with a short one—and when to take off running after a fly ball is caught.

Sending a runner home is the big decision for a Third base coach. In fact, sometimes his job can depend on it. Yankees owner George Steinbrenner once publicly and loudly demoted a third base coach, Mike Ferraro, for sending a man home who got caught at the plate. This said nothing at all about Ferraro's skills, of course, but did once again demonstrate Steinbrenner's crudeness of spirit and pathetic ignorance of the way baseball is played. When a runner is heading for third, the coach has three choices: tell him to come in standing up, tell him to slide, or wave him home. To tell him to stand and stop, he'll hold his left hand up like a traffic cop, point to third base with his right hand, and shout "Hold up here!" making sure that he's in a position where the runner can see him easily. Some coaches can get pretty dramatic about it: You'll sometimes see a coach throw himself on his stomach and pound the ground with both hands to indicate that the runner should slide, or windmill his arm around, run down the baseline, and point to home plate, all the while yelling "Score! Score! Score!" to communicate his desire to see the runner go home. Decisions have to be arrived at quickly here, and a third base coach will occasionally change his mind: He's windmilling the guy home, when suddenly he shouts for him to hold up and dive back into third base.

YERRR OUT!

Did you ever notice that umpires are good dressers? Even the ones who could afford to lose a little weight have uniforms that fit well and are very neat, clean, and freshly pressed. For a while, umpires in the American League wore sports jackets, natty red ones; but then

> *"Baseball is almost the only orderly thing in a very unorderly world. If you get three strikes, even the best lawyer in the world can't get you off."*
> —BILL VEECK

they thought they looked a little too much like Captain Kangaroo, so they got rid of them. But you'll never see an umpire without a good sharp crease in his pants, a crisp shirt collar, and new-looking footwear. This is no accident. Every umpire knows that dressing the part is important—it makes him look like a professional who knows what he's doing, and that's always a good place to start with major league players and managers. The leagues pay for umpires' uniforms, and the nice new shoes are provided by a shoe manufacturer, Pony Shoes, in exchange for an endorsement from the Major League Baseball Umpires' Association.

Since 1952, the major leagues have used four umpires for each game, one at each base and one at home plate. The plate umpire has to make upwards of 250 decisions in every game—at least one for every ball or strike, plus whatever safe/out, foul ball, interference, and other calls he has to make. Calling balls and strikes is difficult. The ball is moving very fast and judging its position accurately takes practice. But the umpire is in a better position than either the batter or the catcher to know what's a strike and what isn't. The catcher is concentrating on catching the ball, the batter on picking it up halfway to the plate so he can hit it. The umpire, on the other hand, has an extra split second to watch the pitch all the way home and then make a judgment.

Umpires must have good visual acuity—the ability to see things clearly from a distance. They also need excellent depth perception and the ability to follow fast-moving objects with their eyes without having to move their bodies. Umpires can wear glasses—their vision has to be correctable to 20/20—but if an umpire needs lenses, he'll probably choose contacts, just to avoid the most obvious way for players or fans to try to get his goat.

Most umpires have their routine before a game—doing a few exercises, getting a drink or something to eat, and so on. Before major league games, umpires must rub up a supply of baseballs to take the gloss off them. Joe Brinkman, a longtime American League umpire who runs a school for aspiring umpires in the off-season, says that the special major league Delaware River mud used for this purpose is nice, but that mud from the bottom of a puddle near the field will probably do just as well.

The umpire seems quite definitive, as all good umpires must be. Lou Brock is safe, no doubt about it. *National Baseball Library & Archive, Cooperstown, NY*

There is always a meeting at the plate before every game, which includes the umpires and both teams' managers and/or coaches. This meeting is used to discuss ground rules, just to remind everyone of what special quirks this particular stadium may have. Even if everyone has been over this before, it doesn't hurt to clarify it once more. And this is the time when managers hand the umpire the written lineup for the game. After the umpire-in-chief—the home plate umpire—gets the lineup cards from the manager, all decisions about everything pertaining to the game, on and off the field, are in the domain of the umpire-in-chief. If he thinks the music on the public address system is too loud, he can tell them to turn it down. If he sees a hot dog vendor's merchandise hanging over the edge of the fence in fair territory, he can make him move it. If it rains, it is his decision to stop play or continue.

It is the umpire's job to make sure that the game proceeds at a good brisk pace, and he can tell players to hurry it up if he thinks it's necessary. Umpires vary in the amount of patience they'll exercise in waiting for a player to get into the box and start hitting or for a pitcher to stop staring and throw the ball.

Umpires make their calls in various dramatic ways, shouting "Steeeeeriiike!!" loud enough to be heard in the next zip code, pulling their fists up and down dramatically, taking long strides and jabbing the air repeatedly with the right arm just to indicate a simple called strike. Why all the theatrics? This is called *selling the call*. Any statement can be made more convincing by vivid pantomime and a modest elevation in volume. You'll notice that the closest calls are often the loudest and most emphatic. These are the calls on which the umpire has to convince all concerned that he is absolutely right and that he saw the play better than anyone else in the park. It is not an accident or a personal quirk, but a well-thought-out plan to keep the game under control and confidence in the umpire high. Because it works, umpires keep doing it—even if people sometimes make fun of them for it.

Once an umpire makes a call, he never changes it. So why do managers argue with umpires? There's a psychological game at work here. No umpire is perfect, and most know when they've made a mistake or when a call could have gone either way. When a manager gets in an umpire's face, he's really arguing for the next close call, which he hopes will go his way. Of course, umpires are on guard. They consciously try never to "even things up" by making two bad calls, one against each team. The rule book, in fact, reminds them of this: "You are no doubt going to make mistakes," it says, addressing the umpire, "but never attempt to 'even up' after having made one."

But umpires are human, too, and every manager hopes that his argument will eventually have its effect.

What does an umpire say or do when a manager or player starts to argue with him? Fans rarely get to hear the actual words (unless they can read lips, or it's a real blow torch like Baltimore's former manager Earl Weaver, who could sometimes be heard even in the cheap seats). Joe Brinkman offers the following advice, and the best umpires follow it. First, the umpire will listen to the complaint. It

"Keep your eye everlastingly on the ball while it is in play," The Book instructs umpires. This umpire has taken the lesson to heart. Even through a cloud of dust, he knows where he's supposed to be looking. *National Baseball Library & Archive, Cooperstown, NY*

doesn't help to refuse to listen—that just makes people angrier. He'll be polite: "I saw the play perfectly, and the runner was safe." Since the outcome is known—the umpire will win the argument—he'll try not to get drawn into a long discussion. The ump will also try to

Our Candidate for the Umpires' Hall of Fame

On September 2, 1972, in Wrigley Field in Chicago, Cubs pitcher Milt Pappas had a perfect game with two outs in the top of the ninth inning. The score was 8–0, and there was a 3–2 count on the batter. On the next pitch, umpire Bruce Froemming called ball 4.

avoid getting ganged up on by a player and his manager or coach— "One at a time, or I can't hear" is a useful phrase to remember. Finally, after a sufficient amount of time has passed, the umpire will say something like, "OK, you've had your say. Now let's play ball." Usually this is enough to end it. Sometimes it isn't. Some managers insist on going further and occasionally getting into personal characterization. Brinkman says that in the big leagues, umpires will allow a manager to say they made a "horseshit call," but will not allow themselves or their ancestors to be similarly characterized. If this happens, the offender will be on his way to the showers.

So what if the umpire throws the manager out of the game, but he refuses to leave? The quick answer is that it never happens, so don't worry about it. But if it ever did happen, the umpire could declare a forfeit and end the game right there. Of course, this is the kind of atomic bomb that no umpire ever wants to use.

Umpires don't like it when a catcher turns around to argue a call—they consider this being shown up. If a catcher has an objection, he's better off voicing it without facing the umpire. The same, as a rule, goes for batters. If they turn to argue a strike call, an ejection can come pretty quickly. Gestures—for example, showing the ump and everyone else in the ballpark how high or how outside the ball was—are similarly frowned upon.

Umpires will tolerate discussion from some players more than from others. Veterans who've earned the right to complain are usually given wider latitude than a rookie who decides to get into an argument. "Shut up and get back in the box, bush" is a likely response to a first-year player who has the temerity to question the judgment of an experienced major league umpire. It has been said that hitters who are known to have a good eye—that is, who rarely strike out—get the benefit of the doubt more than other hitters. At least that's what pitchers always say. Ted Williams supposedly enjoyed this privilege, and Don Mattingly, Wade Boggs, and Tony Gwynn are players of recent vintage said to get calls because of their reputations. Jack Morris, a star pitcher for Detroit, Minnesota, Toronto, and Cleveland for eighteen years, admits that pitchers with a reputation will also get the benefit of the doubt from umpires. But he says that when he first came to the big leagues and faced Carl Yastrzemski, if Yaz didn't swing, it wasn't a strike, even if the ball was right over the plate and belt-high.

> *"I don't think anyone knows what's going on."*
> —DALLAS GREEN, ON REPLACEMENT UMPIRES, 1995

It may appear that being an umpire is easy—all you have to do is have good eyesight and know the rules. But the brief experience of replacement umpires during the umpires' strike at the start of the 1995 season proves otherwise. These guys knew the rules. They'd even umpired some games. But they clearly had no idea how complex, fast, and demanding a major league game can be. One of them made a Little League blunder by disallowing a run scored with two outs, even though the scoring runner crossed the plate before the (nonforced) out was made. Another made an outlandish interference call that cost a team a ball game. A third wrote down some substitutions incorrectly in his lineup card, causing a chain-reaction disaster which he tried to repair by ordering the pitcher to bat twice in a row. Balls and strikes were so inconsistently called that neither batters nor pitchers knew what to expect next. The behavior of the

HOW TO HAVE FUN EVEN THOUGH YOU'RE STUCK IN CLEVELAND

One famous forfeit occurred in Cleveland in 1974, during a never-repeated promotion called "Ten-Cent Beer Night." Nestor Chylack was the unhappy umpire in charge when 25,000 drunken fans charged onto the field to attack Texas Rangers outfielder Jeff Burroughs. Five people were arrested; seven were hurt; and Texas was declared the winner of the game (which, in case anyone still cares, was tied at the time).

manager under these circumstances was predictable: When one of these strange calls went against him, he'd leap up, scream foul language, and get thrown out of the game. When one went in his favor, he'd sit on the bench quietly, a perplexed look on his face designed to conceal the wicked satisfaction he was actually feeling. As Don Mattingly put it, "You don't realize until they're gone just how good the regular guys really are." Good umpires, in other words, operate in a world that violates the rules of nature and logic: You can only see them when they're not there.

More Than a Game: Making a Living in Baseball

In 1941, Joe DiMaggio hit safely in 56 consecutive games, a record that still stands today, more than fifty years later. He had 125 RBIs, the best in the league, and batted .357. But when it came time to sign a contract for 1942, the management of the Yankees first warned him that he might have to take a salary cut ("Well," they said irrelevantly, "there's a war on, you know") and then offered him the same money as the previous year. Maybe the Yankees figured that no one could have two years in a row like that, so 1942 was bound to be worse. Yankee management was in a strong position: DiMaggio's contract, like that of every other Major League Baseball player, contained a reserve clause—the Yankees were the only team he could play for unless they said otherwise. So his choice was to play for the salary he was offered or refuse to play. Anyway, that was the way the stars were treated, so you can imagine what happened with ordinary everyday players. Most baseball players of DiMaggio's era—and up through the 1960s, for that matter—had another job during the off-season. Phil Rizzuto, for example, worked in a men's clothing store to make ends meet. Whitey Herzog worked in construction and refereed basketball games. Today, when utility infielders get paid $500,000 a year, it's hard to believe that people once played Major League Baseball for something other than the big money.

However spoiled and overpaid you think today's players are, it's important to remember that baseball's history of labor relations presents a picture almost as ugly as its history of race relations. From the earliest days of organized ball in the late nineteenth century, owners colluded with each other to keep salaries low, contracts favorable, and the all-important reserve clause in full effect. In 1903, the National and American Leagues reached an agreement that survives, much changed and revised over the years, to this day. In those days, owners didn't try to hide behind lawyers—they stated their desires right out in public and in writing. They created the National Commission, which, as its founding document stated, would control the baseball business "by its own decrees . . . enforcing them without the aid of law, and . . . answerable to no power outside its own." Players, in this arrangement, had a choice: They could either play on the owners' terms, or they could drop dead. Owners today probably still feel this way, but they have the common sense not to put it in writing.

In 1912 when the Detroit Tigers went on strike in sympathy with their star Ty Cobb, who had been suspended for fighting with a fan who had taunted him, the owner of the Tigers immediately hired scabs to play for him. They played one game, losing to Philadelphia 24–2. Then the head of the American League, Ban Johnson, fined each of the Detroit players $50 and ordered them back to work. Charles Comiskey, the owner of the Chicago White Sox, promised star pitcher Ed Cicotte a $10,000 bonus if he won 30 games in 1919. After his 29th victory, with three weeks left in the season, Comiskey benched him for the rest of the year. In 1920, the owners hired a second-rate, frequently reversed red-baiting Chicago judge, Kenesaw

Mountain Landis, as commissioner to give their sport respectability after the 1919 Black Sox scandal. Landis had previously said, in open court, that "I am shocked because you call playing baseball 'labor,'" so the owners knew pretty well where he stood on the question of employee relations. Landis was paid $50,000 a year for *his* labor—roughly twenty times the average player's salary at the time—and he didn't give up his seat on the federal bench for another year, so he collected that salary of $7,500 until the Senate threatened to impeach him if he didn't quit on his own. If the balance of power between players and owners has altered somewhat over the years, the labor strife has not: Since 1970, there has been a strike or a lockout every time the contract between the League of Professional Baseball Clubs and the Major League Baseball Players Association has expired.

Over the years, various attempts were made to form players associations or unions. In 1914, striking players actually formed a league of their own, called the Federal League. The league had no reserve clause, and players were free to negotiate their own contracts, so many players jumped to the new league. Back in the two other major leagues, salaries began to rise with the new competition. Eventually, the Federal League sued Major League Baseball for denying it access to the player pool, but the suit was soon settled, with Federal League owners getting about $600,000 in compensation from Major League Baseball and then dissolving their league. Some of the Federal League owners became major league owners. Among them was Phil Wrigley, and Wrigley Field still stands as a monument to the Federal League, for one of whose teams that stadium was built.

> "Baseball, like some other sports, poses as a sacred institution dedicated to the public good, but it is actually a big, selfish business with a ruthlessness that many big businesses would never think of displaying."
>
> —JACKIE ROBINSON

It was shortly after the dissolution of the Federal League that the Supreme Court confirmed Major League Baseball's belief that it was a game, not a business, and therefore not subject to ordinary antitrust law. This ensured that for the next half-century, baseball players would work in a state of indentured servitude, to be traded from one team to another whether they liked it or not, sold for cash when expedient, and able to sell their services to only one team. Major League Baseball worked hard to maintain this windfall for owners, contending that the reserve clause was essential to competitive balance in the league—without it, they claimed, the richer teams would buy up all the best players. In fact, that's exactly what happened anyway. Richer teams bought better players, and poorer teams had to sell them to stay in business. In the forty-four seasons between 1921 and 1964, the Yankees, the richest team in the richest baseball market, finished first in the league 29 times and second 7 times, and they did it by spending lavishly to buy players from other teams. Of course, the Yankee management's spending benefited other owners (and themselves), not players, and the reserve clause clearly did absolutely nothing to preserve "competitive balance." But the myth of the necessity for the reserve clause was powerful, not only among owners and their loyal following in Congress and the courts, but even among players themselves. In 1951, dozens of players, in a monumental misunderstanding of their self-interest, testified before Congress that the reserve clause was essential to the survival of the national pastime.

> *"I thought baseball was a sport when I became commissioner. I was mistaken. The semi-bandits own it."*
>
> —HAPPY CHANDLER

In 1954, the players formed the Major League Baseball Players Association. This wasn't really a labor bargaining unit, but it did get the owners to agree to put 60 percent of the television revenue from the All-Star Game and the World Series into a players' pension fund. It also got the minimum salary raised to $6,000. The MLBPA had a legal counsel named Robert Cannon, a judge whose ambition it was to be commissioner of baseball—in other words, he longed to work for the owners. He told Congress in 1964 that "we have it so good we don't know what to ask for next." Clearly, he was the kind of labor representative baseball owners could love. And love him they did: When he was offered the job as the first executive director of the MLBPA, the owners voted to take 35 percent of the profits from the All-Star Game and use it to pay for a New York office for him. But he turned down the offer. Instead, the job went to one Marvin Miller, a labor negotiator with extensive experience in the steel industry, and a baseball owner's worst nightmare. He started slowly— with an agreement in 1968 that raised the minimum salary to $10,000 and stipulated the establishment of a joint committee of owners and players to study the reserve clause. But by the time he was done, he had revolutionized baseball labor relations.

Minimum salaries and contributions to the players' pension fund were important in the ensuing contract negotiations, but each time a contract came up for renewal, no issue was more significant than the reserve clause. Curt Flood, a St. Louis Cardinals outfielder, had unsuccessfully challenged the reserve clause in 1970 after he protested a trade to the Phillies, and now free agency was the primary issue in every discussion. In 1972, the owners offered to give free agency to any player who had five years' experience and whose team offered him less than $30,000, or who had eight years' experience and whose team offered him less than $40,000. As the economist Andrew Zimbalist puts it in his book *Baseball and Billions*, "This kind of bargaining made for long strikes." But Miller knew that you don't get everything at once, so he settled for salary arbitration and a grievance procedure—major concessions from the owners that they have been trying to take back ever since—and left the reserve clause alone. He also got them to agree to the "10 and 5" rule. This allows players with ten years' experience, five with one team, to veto trades.

> JUSTICE BLACKMUN EXPLAINS THE LEGAL CONCEPT OF
> THE ESTABLISHED ABERRATION (SOMETIMES KNOWN AS
> NORMAL ABNORMALCY). DO NOT READ THIS WITHOUT
> YOUR LAWYER PRESENT:
>
> *"Professional baseball is a business . . . and thus normally sub-
> ject to federal business law. But it is in a very distinct sense an
> exception and an anomaly. The aberration is an established one."*
>
> —FROM THE MAJORITY SUPREME COURT OPINION UPHOLDING BASEBALL'S
> RESERVE CLAUSE, 1972

The grievance and arbitration agreements were the opening the players needed. First Catfish Hunter grieved a contract with Charlie Finley of the Oakland A's, won his case (Finley had signed a contract promising to pay $50,000 into an insurance annuity for Hunter and then refused to do so), and was made a free agent after the 1974 season. He quickly signed a lucrative deal with the Yankees. Then it really hit the fan: Dave McNally of the Expos and Andy Messersmith of the Dodgers both refused to sign new contracts, played out a year without one, and, claiming they had played out their option year, declared themselves free agents. The owners, of course, maintained that the one-year option was automatically renewed every year—that it was, in effect, a perpetual option. Messersmith and McNally, with Miller's support, objected. Their position was upheld by the arbitrator, Peter Seitz, who believed that the words "one year" did not mean "forever." This made the owners so angry that they fired him and then appealed the decision through the courts. The owners lost. Having been told by one arbitrator and two separate federal courts that they couldn't have their way, they threw a fit and locked out the players at the beginning of spring training in 1976. Eventually, they were persuaded—by their own commissioner—to open up and begin the season; but a new agreement wasn't signed until July, and this agreement made free agency a fact of baseball life: The details are a bit involved, but essentially players with six years' tenure were henceforth free agents, able to sell their skills to whoever wanted to pay for them. Player salaries soared.

The negotiation that led to the strike and the infamous split season of 1981 revolved around the issue of giving compensation to teams whose players became free agents. By the time the strike was over (exactly seven days before the owners' strike insurance ran out), the formula for compensating teams for free agents wasn't much different from the players' original proposal. Essentially, any team that signed a Type A free agent (one whose performance, measured by various agreed-upon statistical criteria, put him in the top 30 percent of all players) would have to put all but twenty-four of its players in a pool, from which the team that lost the free agent could pick a player. (This is how the Mets lost Tom Seaver to Chicago after the 1983 season.) Teams that did not sign Type A free agents could protect more players; teams that agreed to sign none for three years could protect all their players.

In 1985, armed with a newly signed national TV contract that quadrupled their revenue, the owners began the negotiation by claiming that twenty-two of the twenty-six teams were losing money. This required them to open their books, which showed a $42 million loss. The MLBPA hired an economist who went over the books and came up with a $9 million profit. George Steinbrenner was writing off losses on a hotel in Tampa against the Yankees. Anheuser-Busch wasn't counting concession revenue for the Cardinals as baseball income. They had listed it, perfectly legally, as separate income for Busch Stadium. Other teams had other more or less legitimate accounting gimmicks to show how they'd lost millions. Whoever was right, this little exercise showed the value of "open" books when it comes to the finances of Major League Baseball teams. In any case, by this time free agents' salaries were more than the owners were willing to bear, and, under the guidance of a new commissioner, Peter Ueberroth, they decided to do something about it. Unfortunately, what they decided to do was illegal. They colluded with each other to sign free agents at lower salaries or to refuse to sign them at all. Representing hundreds of free agents, the MLBPA dragged them in front of an arbitrator (not once, but three separate times, as the owners kept varying their method of collusion, trying to find one that might work) and each time they were found guilty as charged. They had to pay the MLBPA $280 million in damages.

The 1990 negotiations started with a lockout that began in spring training that year and lasted thirty-two days. The owners wanted a salary cap and an end to salary arbitration. They backed off on both demands, although the qualifying requirements for salary arbitration were made slightly more strict. The new agreement raised the minimum salary to $100,000 with a cost of living increase in 1992. This basic agreement expired in 1994, and the owners' renewed demands for a salary cap quickly led to a strike beginning in August that ended the 1994 season and eliminated the playoffs and World Series. In justifying their demand for a salary cap, the owners played the same old "competitive balance" tune, this time with the variation that smaller-market teams were suffering financial hardship, unable to pay for high-priced free agent talent. They could hardly complain that there was a lack of competitive balance on the field. In fact, in the first seventeen World Series since 1977, when free agency began, thirteen different teams won, and eighteen different teams participated. The owners wanted to pay players less so that they could keep more of the money. This was not unnatural. Nor was it unnatural when the players refused to go along with the idea. The players insisted that the owners had abandoned negotiations without bargaining in good faith, and once again, the courts agreed with the players. It was under this court order against the owners that the players ended their strike and returned to work under the old work rules in April 1995, too late to have a complete season, but early enough to play about 140 games.

AGREEING, BASICALLY

The Basic Agreement between the American and National Leagues of Professional Baseball Clubs and the Major League Baseball Players Association is a legal document more than 100 pages long. You would think that reading such a thing would create the same feelings caused by reading your insurance policies in rapid succession, but a fan would find some of it interesting, and it is quite compelling for anyone who makes his living in the professional baseball business. It outlines, in great and specific detail, the rights and responsibilities baseball players and baseball clubs have toward each other.

One of the first things the agreement refers to is the Uniform Player's Contract, which is attached to the document. This is the boilerplate from which all contracts are written. It does many things besides specify salary. It makes the player agree to allow his picture to be taken and used for promotional purposes by the club. It prohibits him from engaging in boxing or professional wrestling and makes him promise that he won't participate in rough sports or go skydiving, auto racing, or skiing, among other things, without the club allowing him to do so in writing. It makes him promise that he'll keep himself in top physical condition, obey the club's training rules, and "conform to high standards of personal conduct, fair play and good sportsmanship." And it has the two parties to the contract agree that the player "has exceptional and unique skill and ability as a baseball player; that his services to be rendered hereunder are of a special, unusual and extraordinary character which give them peculiar value which cannot be reasonably or adequately compensated for in damages at law, and that the Player's breach of this contract will cause the Club great and irreparable injury and damage." Owners apparently see no contradiction between this clause and their conviction that "replacement players" are a wonderful idea in case there's a strike.

The agreement specifies that the season is 162 games long. And, of course, it also specifies the League Championship Series and the World Series as post-season play. There are complicated regulations about the times games can be scheduled, number of games between open days, doubleheaders and when they can be played, rained-out game rescheduling, and other such matters.

The minimum salary in the 1990 agreement was set at $100,000, and there's a rule forbidding salaries to be cut by more than 20 percent of the previous year's salary. If a player is injured while playing or gets fired because he's not good enough, he still gets paid for the rest of the year. Salary arbitration is permitted to all players with three or more years of major league experience and to some with two years' experience. The major leagues use "final offer arbitration"—that is, the club comes in with its figure, the player comes in with his, and the arbitrator picks one figure or the other, nothing in between. The system encourages negotiation, which is its intent. Owners have won slightly more than half of all arbitrations, but they still hate the provision.

Players are guaranteed first-class travel and accommodations when they are on the road and when they are traveling to spring training and back home at the end of the season. The agreement says that if there aren't enough first-class seats on a commercial airplane, the club has to provide three coach seats for every two players and first-class meals. So if you ever wind up on an airplane sitting next to a professional baseball player, and he's having the steak and champagne while you're sitting there with one of those compartmentalized plastic plates, half apple sauce, half mystery meat, and all at room temperature, that's the explanation. The 1990 per diem meal allowance was set at $54, with cost of living increases in succeeding years. There's also an allowance for days spent in spring training camp. Clubs have to pay moving expenses if they trade a player to another team.

THE POST-SEASON: ONE REASON BASEBALL PLAYERS LIKE TO WIN

Used to be there were eight teams in each league, one pennant winner in each league, and a seven-game World Series. Then came expansion in the number of teams. Then came more expansion and the separation of each league into two divisions, with a playoff between the divisions to decide the league championship. And now comes still more expansion in the number of teams and the separation of each league into three divisions with still more play-offs to decide the division winner and the league winner before the World Series starts.

Four teams get into the Division Series in each league: the winner of each of the three divisions plus a "wild card" team—the team with the best winning percentage apart from the three division winners. There are ways of breaking ties, most of which involve comparing season records against each other of the two tied teams, and some of which involve single-game playoffs. The rules are so complicated that you need a lawyer and two mathematicians to read them for you, so we won't get into it here. We figure we'll just wait until it happens and then try to figure it out. Anyway, here's how it worked in 1995: The wild-card team plays the division champion with the best record, unless the two teams are from the same division, in a five-game series. The other division champs in each league play one another in a five-game series. Winners of each of these series play each other in a seven-game series. Winner of the seven-game series goes to the World Series. Division and wild-card team \opponents, and which division gets the home-field advantage, will be rotated each year. The wild-card team will never have the home-field advantage for the Division Series or the League Championship Series.

The players who get into post-season play make extra money. Beginning with the 1995 season, here's how it works. The leagues take 60 percent of the gate receipts of the first four games of the League Championship, 60 percent of the gate receipts of the first four games of the World Series, and 80 percent of the receipts of the first three games of the Division Championship Series and they put them in a pool, which they divide as follows:

World Series Winner	36 percent
World Series Loser	24 percent
League Championship Losers (2)	24 percent
Division Series Losers (4)	12 percent
Non-wild-card second-place teams (4)	4 percent

The players then vote as to how to share the money among themselves. For the World Series winner, this is a very large amount of money: In 1993, a winning World Series share for one player was $127,920.77.

With the addition of receipts from the Division Playoff Series, this amount is potentially even larger starting in 1995. Even at the bottom, a player on a non-wild-card second-place team in the new alignment will probably come up with about $4,000 as a bonus at the end of the year—not a fortune, but better than a poke in the eye with a sharp stick.

TRADES

In general, teams are free to trade players by assigning their contracts to other teams. This can be done at any time, and the consent of the player is not necessary. But there are exceptions, the main one being for the "10 and 5" players—those with ten years' major league experience, five with one club. These players must give their written consent before their contracts can be assigned. Players who have five or more years' experience can't have their contracts assigned to the minors without their written consent, but they can be assigned to other major league teams. Players who refuse assignment can declare themselves free agents and go out and make their best deal.

FREE AGENCY

Attaining free agency was probably the single most important accomplishment during the years when Marvin Miller headed the MLBPA. At the end of six years of major league experience, every player is a free agent. All he has to do is notify the Player Relations Committee (the owners' group) within a certain period of time after the end of the season. The rest of the involved rules pertaining to free agency are the result of the constant battle between players on the one hand, who want to make free agency as free as possible, and owners on the other, who want to restrict it as much as possible.

If a team loses a Type A free agent, that team is entitled to compensation in the form of draft choices given up by the signing club. This makes signing free agents slightly more expensive—you have to give up a prospect to do it. Teams are limited also in the number of free agents they are allowed to sign in a given year. This number changes according to the number of players who declare themselves free agents that year. When there are fourteen or fewer Type A and B free agents (B's rank in the upper 50 percent, but lower than the upper 30 percent in skill), no club can sign more than one of them. If there are between fifteen and thirty-eight, no club can sign more than two; if there are between thirty-nine and sixty-two, no more than three can be signed by any one club. Type C free agents—those who rank in the lower 50 percent—can be signed by anyone in any numbers.

Free agency involves some other wrinkles as well. For example, a player with five years' major league experience can demand to be traded—to have his contract assigned to another club.

Moreover, he can designate up to six teams that he *doesn't* want to be assigned to. If the club fails to assign his contract within a certain time period, he becomes a free agent. Thus certain players, unhappy at being forced to sit on the bench, can scream "Play me or trade me!" and be sure that they'll be listened to. On the other hand, players can waive this right by signing "no-trade" contracts—contracts that forbid the club from trading them. Players with three years' experience can refuse outright assignment to the minors and declare themselves free agents. Any player, regardless of experience, whose contract is assigned outright to the minor leagues for a second time can also elect free agency instead of going back down to the bush leagues. This doesn't cover players kept on the forty-man major league roster who are sent back and forth to the minor leagues for various reasons—it only applies when the contract is assigned outright to the minor league team.

OWNERS AGREEING WITH EACH OTHER

In addition to the long legal document describing the relationship of the Major League Players Association to the major league teams, there is another equally long document delineating the relationship of major league teams to each other and that of the National and American Leagues to each other. We asked Major League Baseball—the owners' group—to send us a copy. Someone there told us it was a private document that we weren't allowed to see. So we asked the Players Association for it, and they mailed us a copy within a week. We read it, and it's hard to know what secrets the owners' representative we talked to thinks the thing contains. It covers all sorts of stuff, from rules about using standard contract forms to setting up and carrying out the World Series games. Most of it is, as you might have guessed, both intensely boring and completely irrelevant to how the game is played on the field. But, as in the Basic Agreement between players and owners, it does contain some material of interest to fans. We've tried to distill it for you here.

If a National Football League team wants to move from one city to another, it can pick up and move. It doesn't have to ask anyone's permission. But baseball teams do. The commissioner has to approve all moves by any major league team, and specific requirements must be met before a team can even apply to move.

Each major league team agrees to a limit of forty players on its roster, twenty-five of whom are allowed to play on the team at any one time. The rules for putting people on the disabled list and activating roster players are outlined here, so that no team can fiddle with the twenty-five-man limit by having players make believe that they're injured. Signing players is not a free-for-all. There are carefully designed rules about how teams can approach high school players or other amateurs. Neither high school nor college students can be signed to either major or minor league contracts while they are still eligible to play for their school teams, and major league teams can be penalized if they try to persuade a player to withdraw from high school or college or transfer to another college to evade this rule.

An amateur free agent draft occurs on or about June 10 every year that allows teams to reserve amateur players for themselves. Alternating each year between leagues, the team with the worst record the previous year gets first pick in the draft. Then the worst team from the other league picks, the second-to-last team from the first league picks, and so on. This alternating finishes with the two best teams picking last. After an amateur is picked by a team, he can either sign with that team or not sign at all, which limits his bargaining power considerably.

You read in the sports pages of a player being "released on waivers," and this is covered in the Major League Rules as well. A team has to ask all the other teams if they want to be assigned a player's contract before they can release him. After a certain time period, if no team has agreed to pick up his contract, the player is officially released, and the team can bring up another player to replace him.

Players can be suspended for insubordination or misconduct, or for not being in physical shape to play. The team can impose fines as well and deduct them from the player's salary. Needless to say, the Players Association has ensured that there are appeal processes for the player who is fined or suspended.

Players can play in Winter Leagues in the countries that have them—mostly in Mexico and the Caribbean—but they can only do so with the permission of the major league team. There are also lots of rules for when and under what circumstances players can play in exhibition games. It is forbidden, for example, for players to play in games scheduled on the days preceding and following the All-Star Game, and players are not allowed to participate in any all-star game except the officially sanctioned one.

The Major League Rules contains a long section on conflict of interest. Owners are not allowed to have an interest in more than one team, either directly or indirectly through stock ownership. This can become a problem where a team is owned by a large corporation whose stock is owned in significant amounts by other owners, though owners, so far as we know, have never found such conflicts insurmountable barriers to ownership.

Rule 21 concerns misconduct. It forbids anyone connected with a club from promising to lose a game or failing to give his best effort to win. It prohibits gifts for defeating a competing club and gifts to umpires. It prohibits betting on any baseball game, with the penalty being ineligibility for one year. If you bet on a game in which you are performing, the penalty is permanent ineligibility. Rule 21 forbids violence or any physical attack on other players or umpires. Even touching an umpire can lead to penalties imposed by the league office, as warranted by the case. A printed copy of Rule 21 must be posted in every clubhouse, just in case anyone has forgotten them.

An agreement to play by uniform rules is also included in the document. Rule 25 sets up the Rules Committee, which meets to consider and vote on changes to the Official Playing Rules. There's a subcommittee of this group that concerns itself with scoring and official records.

The rules for the World Series are included at the end of the document, and they go right down to details about who gets how many free tickets. Each home team has to give 500 tickets for each game to the visiting team, plus five tickets to each eligible player of the visiting team. Each of the other major league clubs gets 100 free tickets to every game. This no doubt prevents a lot of loud arguing every fall.

DOWN ON THE FARM

Players in other national sports leagues have almost all come directly from college. But colleges have never really provided baseball players sufficient experience to go straight into Major League Baseball. This may be because baseball skills develop over longer periods of time—it takes a few years of watching and waiting before you can figure out if a twenty- or twenty-one-year-old is going to grow into major league material. So professional baseball has always had to grow its own, and the major leagues have an extensive system of player development—the minor leagues. This is where young baseball players learn their trade.

There are about 150 minor league teams with affiliations to major league organizations, and a handful of independent teams, including one entire league, recently established, that is made up of only independent teams. All of the teams except the few independents belong to the National Association of Professional Baseball Leagues, which has an agreement with the majors spelling out their relationship.

There are several levels of minor leagues, starting with the rookie league and moving up through Class A, Class AA, and Class AAA. Some Triple A teams—the Buffalo Bisons, for example, which is affiliated with the Cleveland Indians—play almost-major-league-quality baseball in shiny new stadiums in front of almost-major-league numbers of fans. And some play in run-down fields before crowds as small as a few hundred people. The Professional Baseball Agreement obliges the majors to maintain 119 teams, including one Triple-A and one Double-A for each team, plus varying numbers of A-level and rookie league teams. Most teams have six affiliated minor league franchises. The Yankees and Mets each have seven; the Cardinals have eight. With free agency, major league teams can count on needing a player at each position at least every six years and usually more often. So they have to keep the talent coming.

The major league team pays all the salaries of all the players, coaches, and managers and all equipment costs—including bats, balls, uniforms, medical supplies, you name it. About the only thing they don't pay for is travel expenses. In exchange for this, the major league team gets complete control of the players and coaches—it can move them wherever it wants, whenever it wants, and the owners of the minor league teams have nothing to say about such personnel decisions. In a sense, minor league baseball owners are like movie theater owners—they sell the tickets to the movie and then push popcorn and soda, but they don't get any say in decisions about the artistic product itself. The minor league owners make most of their money on ticket sales, but they'd go out of business if they didn't have beer, hot dogs, and souvenirs to sell, too.

All together, there are about 5,500 minor league baseball players at any one time. Of these, about 90 percent will never play in the majors. Of those who do get to the majors, a minority will have significant careers in the bigs—say, five years or longer. Major league teams pay for bats, balls, and salaries for hundreds, even thousands of players before they develop one major leaguer. Some estimate that more than a million dollars is spent to bring just one successful player to the Show.

Almost all major leaguers have put in time in the minors. Of present players, only Dave Winfield, Jim Abbott, and John Olerud have no minor league experience; the other 700 or so all played for farm teams. This has always been true. A few well-known names from baseball history—Frankie Frisch, Catfish Hunter, Sandy Koufax, and others—went straight to the big leagues from college or the sandlots; but most big names—Ruth, Gehrig, DiMaggio, Musial, Mays, Aaron—did their time in the bush leagues.

On all minor league teams except the few independents, the contracts of the players are owned by the major league affiliate. In most cases, an amateur player is drafted by a major league team and then sent to one of the organization's farm teams. There, he either succeeds and moves on to the next level of play or fails and finds a new career. Minor league players can become free agents after six years, but few stay in the minors that long. For most, the minor leagues are a very temporary proposition—it's either up or out, all in the space of a few years.

How many years is "a few"? Both fans and baseball professionals often say something like this: "Kids who come up these days are bigger and stronger, but they haven't spent enough time in the minors to learn the fundamentals of the game." Then everyone nods sagely. Keith Hernandez makes exactly this observation in his book *Pure Baseball*, and many sportswriters routinely say the same thing. But Keith and all the others are dead wrong. Writer Bill James, who often takes the trouble to check up on things that "everyone knows," has proved it. The average number of minor league games played by major league regulars is about 450, and that number has hardly changed at all in the past fifty years. This means that today's major league regulars have spent somewhere between three and four seasons on the farm. The average age at which a major league player has played in 100 games is about 24.5, and that average has been quite steady over the last fifty years, too.

If you hear someone pretending to know what he's talking about by complaining that "these kids don't get their minor league seasoning like they used to," just tell him the facts of life.

During the season, players are sent down to, and back up from, the minor leagues as the team needs them. The major league team can have twenty-five players with the major league team, but forty men on the roster. This means that fifteen roster players are in the minors at all times, available as replacements for injured players, or, if they're good enough, for a permanent place on the team.

In the minors, the pay stinks. The median income for a rookie league player is about $850 a month; for a Class-A player about $1,000; for a Double-A man around $1,500. At the Triple-A level, the median is around $5,000, which is good money, but of course it's only for the five-month season. If a player comes up to play in the majors, he experiences a distinct change in lifestyle: The minimum salary in the bigs is now more than $100,000.

Minor league baseball has grown immensely in fan interest over the past decade, and with good reason. Tickets are cheap; parking is often free; and you get to watch professional baseball played on real grass. The stadiums are small, and you sit close to the action. The players, underpaid though they may be, gladly sign autographs, talk to the fans, and never fail to run out a ground ball or a pop fly. You could do worse, and you probably have.

7

Chatter: How They Talk Baseball, and How You Can Too

Sometimes people talk baseball without even realizing they're doing it. He struck out. He couldn't get to first base with her. That price isn't even in the same ballpark as the quote we got yesterday. He's very loyal, always willing to go to bat for his employees. Be sure you touch all the bases. He started out with two strikes against him. Let's pitch this idea to the client. Three strikes and you're out. Joe couldn't make it today, so I'm pinch-hitting for him. (This one always bothers us—the metaphorical pinch hitter is always a second choice, someone not as good as the other guy. In baseball, of course, a pinch hitter is precisely the opposite—he's better at the job than the originally scheduled hitter. No—we don't think this little lesson in semantics will have any effect whatsoever on American speech, and we fully expect people to go right on using "pinch-hit" the way they always do.) In any case, baseball talk permeates American speech,

191

even that of people who know little or nothing about talking baseball. It's exaggerating—but only a little—to say we've borrowed words and expressions from baseball language just as surely as we've borrowed gesundheit and gestalt, schlep and schmuck, belles lettres and bon voyage, pizza and pianissimo.

If you listen to two baseball fans talking to each other about the game, it does sound in some ways like a foreign language. Which, in a sense, it is. Baseball, like most trades, has both a formal technical language and a slang or jargon that develops and changes over the years. You won't learn to talk baseball by reading this chapter—any more than you learned to talk French by taking three years of it in high school. To speak French without an accent, you have to be born where they speak French, or live there as a child. Same goes for baseball: If you want to really talk baseball—without an accent— you probably have to start talking it when you're under the age of twelve. But just as you can learn to speak and decipher French well enough to get along, even well enough to enjoy yourself a bit, you can learn to understand baseball well enough to increase your enjoyment of the game.

Let's face it: If you're going on a car trip during baseball season, most of the stuff you can tune in to on the radio is third-rate— idiotic talk shows, mindless music, repetitive stories from the all-news station, and amateur commercials starring the owner of the Chevrolet dealership in whatever town you happen to be passing through. But if you tune in to a Major League Baseball game, you're listening to something first-rate: first-rate baseball. For this reason alone, it's worth trying to understand it.

A typical radio broadcaster's style might involve plenty of jargon, abbreviated expressions, even the occasional neologism. This is what he (or she) might sound like describing the Yankees' Scott Kamienicki pitching to John Olerud of the Blue Jays:

Two on, two out, 0–1 to Olerud. No way to pitch this guy. Hits to all fields. Kamienicki deals to Olerud. Change is in for a strike, one and one . . . Olerud holds the bat completely silent.

Opponents batting .195 against Kamienicki this year with runners in scoring position. . . .

Cut on and missed, good breaking pitch, down and away. One and two to Olerud. Olerud now hitting at a .352 pace. Kamienicki sat them down in order for the first two innings, but he had to work his way out of a jam in the third, and here he is getting shelled again in the fourth. Cut on and missed, strike three! High, probably out of the zone. And that does it. At the end of four, Toronto 0, 4, and 0; Yankees 0, 2, and 0.

And that is just part of what he'll say about one batter during a two-and-a-half-hour broadcast—no wonder you're confused. But let's see if we can deconstruct the text here and see what the announcer is really saying.

"Two on, two out." Two on is short for "two men on base." We just tuned in, so we don't know which two bases they're on. And there are two men who've already made out.

"0–1 to Olerud." This is the count—no balls and one strike. When you say what the count is, you always say the number of balls first and then the number of strikes. Even when balls and strikes are mentioned (like this) without the numbers, the phrase is always "balls and strikes," never "strikes and balls." Why? We don't know. Why do you say "a big red house" instead of "a red big house"? You just do.

"No way to pitch this guy." This is what your high school English teacher called *hyperbole*. The announcer is saying that Olerud is a hitter with no obvious weaknesses. You can't throw him one particular kind of pitch and expect to get him out easily. In that sense, there's no specific way to pitch to him—you just have to throw very good pitches.

"Hits to all fields." Olerud doesn't consistently "pull" the ball— that is (for a lefty), hit the ball to right field. And he doesn't consistently "poke" or "slap" it, either—that is, hit to left field. Instead, he hits to all fields, so you never know where the ball is going when he makes contact.

"Kamienicki deals to Olerud." Metaphor, as you have learned to call it. He "deals" in the sense of a dealer in a card game—that is, he offers something to play with, in this case the ball. "Deals" here just means "pitches."

"Change is in for a strike." "Change" is short for change-up, a kind of pitch, described in Chapter 3, that looks like a fastball as it is released, but goes about 10 miles per hour slower. "In for a strike" means that it was in the strike zone, but the batter didn't swing at it. A literal translation might be: "The pitcher threw a pitch that looked like it was going to go faster than it actually did, and it passed through an imaginary rectangle about 2 feet high and 17 inches across, the bottom of which is located about 2 feet off the ground above home plate, but the batter didn't swing his bat to try to hit it, so the umpire called a strike."

"One and one." We know this is balls and strikes, one of each.

"Olerud holds the bat completely silent." Shouldn't that be "silently"? Anyway, some batters wave the bat around while they're waiting for the pitch. Some don't. To "hold the bat completely silent" means to keep the bat perfectly still until you're ready to swing. By extension, a "quiet" hitter is one who doesn't jiggle around while he waits for the pitcher to deliver.

"Opponents batting .195 against Kamienicki this year with runners in scoring position." "Scoring position" refers to second and third base. So now we know that at least one of the runners is on second or third. When Kamienicki finds himself with runners on second and/or third base, hitters apparently don't do too well, getting a hit less than 20 percent of the time. The significance of such a statistic is arguable, but most fans will find it of at least some interest.

"Kamienicki sat them down in order in the first two innings." No Blue Jays got on base in the first two innings. Six men came up to bat, and each one made an out.

"He had to work his way out of a jam in the third." In the third inning, he allowed some people to get on base, but he managed to get three outs before anyone scored.

"Here he is getting shelled." He's allowing multiple hits in one inning.

"Cut on and missed." Olerud swung and didn't hit the ball. To "cut on" a ball or "take a cut" means to swing. The expression "take my cuts" is sometimes used by hitters to mean get some playing time, some practice with the bat, a chance to show what they can do.

"Good breaking pitch, down and away." A breaking pitch, as we know from Chapter 3, is a ball that curves. It could be a curveball, a slider, a screwball, a knuckleball, or any of several variations of these pitches. "Down and away" means that the ball traveled low and outside—away from the batter. The normal trajectory of a curveball thrown by a left-handed pitcher to a left-handed batter would be down and away, so we can assume that Kamienicki has thrown the curve. It was "good" because the batter missed it. If he'd hit it, the announcer would probably have said that the curve "hung"— that is, didn't curve—or that the batter "went down and got it"— that is, reached down and hit it even though it was curving as it was designed to.

There is some dispute over whether an announcer sitting several hundred feet away from the plate can actually make such fine distinctions, but never mind.

"Olerud now hitting at a .352 pace." Picturesque way of telling Olerud's batting average.

"Cut on and missed, strike 3!" See above.

"High, probably out of the zone." Olerud apparently swung at a bad pitch—a pitch that would have been a ball if he hadn't swung. "The zone" is the strike zone, and this pitch was above it.

"And that does it." Three out, and the half-inning is over.

"At the end of four . . ." This is the end of the fourth inning— that is, the home team has batted for the fourth time. If he'd said "at the end of three and a half innings," you would know that the visiting team had batted four times and the home team was about to come up for its fourth chance. Therefore, if you just tuned in, you know that this game is being played in Toronto.

"Toronto 0, 4, and 0; Yankees 0, 2, and 0." The announcer has just told you what the score is and how many hits and errors each team has. On the scoreboard, runs, hits, and errors are always listed in that order. In this game, neither team has scored; the Blue Jays have four hits, the Yankees have two; and neither team has made an error.

The announcer only used about 135 words, but he really said a mouthful.

Announcer talk is probably slightly different from baseball player talk, which may be slightly different again from newspaper sports page talk—different dialects, if you will, of the same language. If you saw the movie *Bull Durham,* you heard a pretty good rendition of baseball player talk. You know, for example, what a Baseball Annie is—we don't have to go into the lurid details. You also know what "the Show" is—in fact, baseball announcers, as far as we can remember, never even used the term before the movie came out. Now everyone uses it. It means, of course, the big leagues, a shortened form, we assume, of "the big show" or some such thing. The Show is where all minor leaguers want to go—where the money is good, the crowds are big, the girls are prettier (it's said), and you get white balls for batting practice instead of the dirt-covered brown ones you have to use in the minors, since the team owners may be only marginally less poverty-stricken than the players.

> *"I feel like I'm on top of the mental aspect, I'm throwing to the right place, running the bases better, I know how many outs there are. . . ."*
> —JACK CLARK

Organized ball is another expression for the professional baseball business, and it's often abbreviated *O.B.* For example, "the worst head in O.B." is the stupidest person in baseball (if you include owners in the pool as well as players, this becomes a very tough call). Because baseball is a game that demands thinking, questioning people's intelligence is a constant. "Have an idea out there!" you may hear a manager yell, meaning "Think! Use your head!"; or, more crudely, "Stop being stupid!" Sometimes a pitcher is accused of "losing it" because his velocity is not what it should be, but if he's "losing it up here," his problem is even more serious.

Pitching and hitting have some of the most picturesque slang, and the number of terms devoted to scaring hitters is impressive. "Keep him honest" or "loosen him up" is the most polite way of advising a pitcher not to let a hitter get away with anything. A pitcher might gently offer a "purpose" pitch—one designed to move the hitter away from the plate; "a little chin music" is a similar pitch, but one that's to terrify. A hitter's best response to a pitcher who gives him some "high cheese" (a high inside fastball) would be to "take him downtown" by hitting a "dinger" (home run). Occasionally, a pitcher who sees no other way out with a batter who is "crowding the plate" (standing too close to it) will "deck him"—make him dive to the ground to avoid being hit by a pitch.

When a pitcher is pitching well, hitters will say he's "throwing seeds up there"—the ball seems small and hard to find. By contrast it looks "big as a grapefruit" when a hitter is hitting well. It's always "big as a grapefruit"—never any other object, however easy it may be to think of things similar in size to that fruit. Hitters like to hit a "frozen rope"—a hard line drive whose trajectory to the outfield is perfectly straight—as opposed to a "blooper," which goes up and then back down in a lazy arc, sometimes easy to catch, but occasionally falling in for a cheap hit—a "Texas leaguer" or a "dunker," dunked in between two fielders, just out of the reach of both. A "Baltimore chop" is a hundred-year-old term still in use—a ball chopped straight down into the ground that bounces high enough in the air to allow the batter to make it to first before the infielder can get his hands on it. It takes its name from the Baltimore team in the National League in the 1890s that invented it as a deliberate tactic (with the aid of a grounds crew that packed the dirt in front of home plate hard as a rock to give the ball a good surface to bounce off).

A hitter wants to avoid "getting under" the ball—hitting it on the lower half of the sphere and popping it up. And he's just as wary of "topping" it, or hitting it on the top half, with a grounder and an out the result. He would of course prefer to hit a grounder "in the hole" where there is no defensive player to catch it, and it can slither into the outfield for a hit. Whereas a power hitter will usually hold his hands at the end of the bat, some hitters "choke up" on the bat—slide their hands up the handle, making the bat easier to swing.

The "heater" is the fastball, and pitchers who throw that pitch well are said to throw "smoke," "heat," or "high gas." When a pitcher "takes something off" the pitch, it means he's throwing an "off-speed" pitch or a "change-up," or the "change," for short. The "scroogie" is a screwball; the "flutterball" is an ancient term for the knuckleball, more often called the "knuckler" today. The curve is "the hook" or "Uncle Charlie," or, for the more picturesque speakers, like Tim McCarver, the Mets' TV announcer, "Lord Charles." The split-finger fastball is the "splitter," not to be confused with the "spitter," which is the illegally moistened pitch described in Chapter 2. The rule book offers the obsolete terms "shine ball," "emery ball," and "mud ball" to describe this pitch. Sometimes it's called, simply, a "wet one." As we know from Chapter 2, a pitcher bent on cheating can cut or scrape a ball to affect its trajectory, but this illegal action should not be confused with the "cut fastball" or "cutter," a perfectly legal variation on the fastball that curves slightly right to left (when thrown by a righty). The "cutting" here refers to the way the wrist is snapped when the ball leaves the pitcher's hand—the wrist is not as sharply twisted as with a curveball.

A pitcher can throw "down and away," as we heard earlier, or "up and in," the opposite. (And of course "up and away" and "down and in," to cover all the points of the compass.) The pitcher wants at all costs to avoid throwing one in the batter's "wheelhouse," where he'll be able to "turn on it"—take a good swing. This area—where the batter can get his best shot at hitting the ball hard—is for some reason also called his "kitchen." Maybe the kitchen is a warm and homey place, which is exactly how the batter will feel when he gets a pitch there. The pitcher can "paint the corners" by throwing strikes that go over the edges of the plate, and he can even throw one "on the black"—so close to the edge of the strike zone that the ball passes over the black outline painted around the edge of home plate. Or he can be "wild"—not get the ball over the plate at all. When he's throwing well, he is said to "have good stuff," but when he isn't, he's "got nothing." When a batter is hit by a pitch, he will rarely grab the spot that was hit or reveal that it might have caused pain—he wants to imply that the pitcher doesn't have good enough stuff even to raise a bump. The more demonstrative batters will yell at the pitcher, "Is that all you got? You got nothing!"

A good runner has "wheels"; a good fielder knows how to "pick it"—make good plays on ground balls, especially the "grass cutters," or fast grounders, and "squibs," the weakly hit grounders that a fielder has to charge toward and scoop up on the run. "Nice pick!" is high praise, and a good fielder is said to have "soft hands," as opposed to the "stone hands" that let a ball bounce off them. Sometimes a "good field, no hit" player is "in there for his glove"—that is, in the lineup because he's good at defense, even though "he couldn't hit water if he fell out of a boat."

Even warming up has its technical terms. Sometimes you see a sign on the wall in back of home plate or elsewhere that says "No Pepper." This has nothing to do with spices—"pepper" is an infield warm-up exercise that, played often enough in the same spot, destroys the grass. There's a coach on every team who is good with a "fungo" bat, the skinny bat designed for hitting warm-up grounders and fly balls to fielders. The coach stands in a dirt circle designed especially for the purpose, flips the ball a few feet in the air, and hits it precisely where he wants it to go, either on the fly or on the ground. There's a precise ritual for this, everyone playing his part perfectly—get to the game an hour early and watch it.

After a hitter makes the first or second out of an inning with no men on base, the infielders throw the ball "around the horn," in another of baseball's traditions. This rapid tossing of the ball from one infielder to another and then back to the pitcher has no function, other than to punctuate the successful play that the team has just made. And there's a specific way it's done, depending on which fielder made the putout. The rule—or, rather, the tradition—is that the ball rotates counterclockwise, and the third baseman always delivers the ball to the pitcher. No one touches the ball twice, except the third baseman. So, for example, when the second baseman makes the putout, you'll see the ball go from him to the shortstop, to the third baseman, to the catcher, to the first baseman, and then all the way across to the third baseman, who flips it to the pitcher. When the putout is made in the outfield, the infielder who receives the throw from the outfielder starts the little game as if he had made the putout. Why do they do this? Because, that's why.

"Babe Ruth is dead. Throw strikes!"

—ADVICE SUPPOSEDLY OFFERED BY MANAGERS TO PITCHERS WHO THROW FANCY BREAKING BALLS TO A WEAK HITTER INSTEAD OF HARD FASTBALLS DOWN THE MIDDLE

A "control pitcher" throws precise strikes and rarely walks anyone. For some reason his control is always called "pinpoint." The pitcher with an overwhelming fastball is a "power pitcher," but those who rely on tricky breaking pitches are "junkballers." The language here expresses a certain amount of contempt, because it's the power pitcher who gets the respect of hitters. Pitchers who "throw junk," even the successful ones, are thought of (at least by hitters) as a lesser breed. Players like to see a power pitcher go straight up against a power hitter. If a power pitcher decides to throw junk to, or "pitch around," a good hitter, players will accuse him of cowardice, and the "bench jockeys" on the offensive team will start yelling insults at him from the dugout. This kind of pitching is sometimes called "nibbling"—nibbling around the edges of the plate instead of throwing heat right down the middle. Occasionally, a pitcher's own teammates will get annoyed if a pitcher with an 0–2 count on a weak hitter starts playing footsie with him instead of "challenging" him with a hard fast one. Sometimes a hitter will "sit on a fastball"— know (or at least be pretty sure) a fastball is coming and be prepared to hit it. Similarly, if a hitter is "looking away," it means he's expecting a pitch on the outside part of the plate. A pitcher who is allowing lots of hits is getting "shelled" or "rocked," and he's liable to be "knocked out," "yanked," "lifted," or "sent to the showers," which all mean pretty much the same thing: He'll be removed from the game— invited to "go grab some bench"—and a new pitcher will take over.

Red Barber, probably the most literate and intelligent announcer ever to work a baseball game, developed a series of picturesque expressions to describe what happens on a baseball field. Here are some examples:

"He's sittin' in the catbird seat." (The pitcher has a big lead.)

"Hold the phone!" (The manager is headed for the pitcher's mound.)

"The fat's in the fire." (A critical moment in the game.)

"They're tearin' up the pea patch." (The team is scoring many runs.)

"Runnin' like a bunny with his tail on fire." (Fast, evidently.)

A "cripple hitter" is a batter who is good at hitting pitchers' mistakes. You can get them out if you pitch well, but hang a curve or let a fastball get too high, and they'll "take a good rip at it" and "wrap it around the flagpole." Dave Kingman, who always seemed to be either striking out or hitting a dinger, was a great cripple hitter.

If you strike out, you've "fanned" or "whiffed"; and if you don't get a hit all day, you've "taken the collar." No hits in three times at bat is "going 0-for-3," an "ofer" for short. When a team makes three outs in a row in an inning without getting anyone on, they are said to have "gone down one-two-three," or to have "gone quietly."

The catcher is sometimes called the "receiver"; third base is "the hot corner"; a shortstop or second baseman is the "pivot man." On the double play, he steps on second to force the runner out, and then pivots to throw to first to get the batter-runner. If the pivot man does this successfully, the team is said to "get two," that is, complete a double play by getting two outs on one batted ball. A base is a "bag" or a "sack," and a second baseman is a "second sacker," at least in the sports page cliché, if not in the spoken language of a real baseball player. A runner who is on base can be "picked off" or "erased"—caught off base by a throw from the pitcher or catcher. Sometimes such a throw will catch the runner in a "rundown"— stuck between two bases while two infielders hunt him down by throwing the ball between them, forcing him to run back and forth in a (usually futile) effort to avoid the tag.

> *"I firmly believe that the most extraordinary human game is baseball, that it is a twelve-month endeavor, and it deeply occupies the mind and heart even when not being played. It's a game that you play in the silence of the night."*
>
> —JONATHAN SCHWARTZ, NEW YORK WRITER AND RADIO PERSONALITY

It's not easy, but it can be learned. As with any language, you'll know you're speaking it well enough when you can do it without having to think about it. And when you start dreaming in baseball language, you've got it.

Bibliography

In case you haven't noticed, there are a lot of baseball books out there. This is a list of ones I've found interesting and useful. It does not pretend to be complete or systematic.

Acton, Jay, with Nick Bakalar. *Green Diamonds: The Pleasures and Profits of Investing in Minor League Baseball*. New York: Zebra Books, 1993.

Adair, Robert. *The Physics of Baseball*. New York: HarperCollins, 1990.

Angell, Roger. *Once More Around the Park: A Baseball Reader*. New York: Ballantine Books, 1992.

The Baseball Encyclopedia, 9th edition. New York: Macmillan, 1993.

Bass, Mike. *Marge Schott: Unleashed*. Champaign, IL: Sagamore Publications, 1993.

Bavasi, Buzzie, with John Strege. *Off the Record*. Chicago: Contemporary Books, 1987.

Bouton, Jim. *Ball Four Plus Ball Five: An Update 1970–1980*. New York: Stein and Day, 1981.

Brinkman, Joe, and Charlie Euchner. *The Umpire's Handbook*. Lexington, MA: The Stephen Greene Press, 1987.

Cataneo, David. *Peanuts and Crackerjacks: A Treasury of Baseball Legends and Lore*. Nashville: Rutledge Hill Press, 1991.

Charlton, James, ed. *The Baseball Chronology*. New York: Macmillan, 1991.

Cluck, Bob. *Play Better Baseball*. Chicago: Contemporary Books, 1993, 1994.

Dewey, Donald, and Nicholas Acocella. *Encyclopedia of Major League Baseball Teams*. New York: HarperCollins, 1993.

Durso, Joseph. *Baseball and the American Dream*. St. Louis: Sporting News, 1986.

Falkner, David. *Nine Sides of the Diamond*. New York: Times Books, 1990.

Fiffer, Steve. *How to Watch Baseball*. New York: Facts on File, 1987.

Filichia, Peter. *Professional Baseball Franchises*. New York: Facts on File, 1993.

Fraser, Ron, *Championship Baseball*. North Palm Beach, FL: The Athletic Institute, 1983.

Golenbock, Peter. *Bums: An Oral History of the Brooklyn Dodgers*. New York: Putnam, 1984.

Gould, Stephen Jay. *The Flamingo's Smile: Reflections on Natural History*. New York: Norton, 1985.

Halberstam, David. *Summer of '49*. New York: William Morrow, 1989.

Hernandez, Keith, and Mike Bryan. *Pure Baseball*. New York: HarperCollins, 1994.

Herzog, Whitey, and Kevin Horrigan. *White Rat: A Life in Baseball*. New York: Harper & Row, 1987.

Honig, Donald. *Baseball America: The Heroes of the Game and the Times of Their Glory*. New York: Macmillan, 1985.

James, Bill. *The Bill James Baseball Abstract*. New York: Ballantine Books, 1982–1988.

Kindall, Jerry. *Baseball: Play the Winning Way*. New York: Sports Illustrated, 1993.

Koppett, Leonard. *The Man in the Dugout*. New York: Crown Publishers, 1993.

Koppett, Leonard. *The New Thinking Fan's Guide to Baseball*. New York: Simon & Schuster, 1991.

McCarver, Tim. *Oh, Baby, I Love It!* New York: Villard Books, 1987.

Nathan, David H. *Baseball Quotations*. New York: Ballantine Books, 1991.

Nemec, David. *The Rules of Baseball*. New York: Lyons & Burford, 1994.

Official Baseball Rules. St. Louis: Sporting News, 1995.

Okrent, Daniel, and Steve Wulf. *Baseball Anecdotes*. New York: Oxford University Press, 1989.

Pascarelli, Peter. *The Toughest Job in Baseball: What Managers Do, How They Do It, and Why It Gives Them Ulcers*. New York: Simon & Schuster, 1993.

Petroff, Tom, with Jack Clary. *Baseball Signs and Signals*. Dallas: Taylor Publishing, 1986.

Quigley, Martin. *The Crooked Pitch: The Curveball in American Baseball History*. Chapel Hill, NC: Algonquin Books, 1988.

Reichler, Joseph L. *The Great All-Time Baseball Record Book*. New York: Macmillan, 1993.

Seaver, Tom, with Lee Lowenfish. *The Art of Pitching*. New York: Hearst Books, 1984.

Skolnik, Richard. *Baseball and the Pursuit of Innocence*. College Station: Texas A&M University Press, 1994.

Thorn, John, and John Holway. *The Pitcher*. New York: Prentice Hall, 1987.

Thorn, John, and Pete Palmer. *Total Baseball*, 3d edition. New York: HarperCollins, 1993.

Thrift, Syd, and Barry Shapiro. *The Game According to Syd: The Theories and Teachings of Baseball's Leading Innovator*. New York: Simon & Schuster, 1990.

Wagonner, Glen, Kathleen Mooney, and Hugh Howard. *Baseball by the Rules*. Dallas: Taylor Publishing, 1987.

Will, George F. *Men at Work*. New York: Macmillan, 1990.

Williams, Dick, and Bill Plaschke. *No More Mr. Nice Guy: A Life of Hardball*. San Diego: Harcourt Brace Jovanovich, 1990.

Zimbalist, Andrew. *Baseball and Billions*. New York: Basic Books, 1992.

Index